WF299

GW01191935

FAST
Whole Food

By the same author

COOKING NATURALLY
IMPOSSIBLE-TO-RESIST DESSERTS

FAST

Whole Food

Healthy Meals
in Under 40 Minutes

MARIA MIDDLESTEAD

HODDER AND STOUGHTON
AUCKLAND LONDON SYDNEY TORONTO

Copyright © 1988 Maria Middlestead
First published 1988
Reprinted 1989, 1990
ISBN O 340 426853

All rights reserved. No part of this publication may be reproduced or transmitted
in any form or by any means, electronic or mechanical including photocopy,
recording, or any information storage and retrieval system, without permission
in writing from the publisher.

Typeset by Acorn Graphics Ltd, Auckland.
Printed and bound by Singapore National Printers Ltd for Hodder &
Stoughton Ltd, 44-46 View Road, Glenfield, Auckland, New Zealand.

Contents

Introduction

FRESH FOOD WITH A FRESH IMAGE

Commonly, wholefood is given a mean image. Something eminently commendable — like cold showers — but often as neatly avoided. There are images of gingham and pottery. Naked brown rice and the lingering after-effect of too many lentils. Lengthy hours of preparation and monastic ritual. Soaking, sprouting, tending, tiring.

But the term wholefood simply refers to the fresh whole seasonal unrefined provender nature generously provided us with. Food which needs less complementation than something frozen, packaged or preservatised into eternal shelf-life.

Wholefood is the cornerstone of nouvelle cuisine and all edible art, and a crucial building block to a vital and vigorous lifestyle. Sadly, wholefood has been promoted as health sustaining often to the unnecessary exclusion of elements like glamour and sensuality, simplicity and finesse, leaving the diner fit for little but terminal tedium.

No longer need this be the case. Wholefood can be fast food. Creative and nourishing food. So put on your apron and your sneakers, set your alarm, and get ready for a fun, fast-paced adventure in the kitchen.

Within this book is a series of complete meals each fully outlined with imaginative variations given for completely vegetarian cuisine and for using fish, chicken and other meats.

There are sections on Appetisers and Desserts and tips on presentation so that any of these menus can easily be rounded out for elegant entertaining. Also, because of their speed and simplicity the menus are readily suited to those cooking for one.

Never again do I wish to hear, "I'd love to cook more wholefood meals but they take too much time." They needn't, you needn't, and this book shows how.

Marla Middlestead

TIPS FOR SPEED AND COMFORT

- First, read all of these introductory pages and the Cook's Helper section at the back of the book! Speed can mean exuberant efficiency or harried haste. The time-honoured dictum of making sure that all your ingredients are on hand is just as applicable to "ingredients" like planning, cooking techniques' awareness, and nutritional know-how.
- A little work planning in your mind saves you from a large amount of stress and unnecessary time fluffing about in your kitchen later on. There is nothing more anxiety — if not disaster — prone than arriving home late and thinking, "What the heck am I going to cook?" Then perhaps starting on a menu only to find one or more crucial ingredients missing.

  Try for a few minutes on a Sunday or the day before you go food shopping, to consider the week ahead. Or at least set aside some time the day or morning before to plan the evening's meal and make sure you have the necessary foodstuffs. All this saves more time than it takes.
- Feel physically comfortable and enjoy yourself! This may sound simplistic but take the time if necessary to change your shoes and clothes, even have a quick shower, maybe pour yourself a glass of wine, put on some fine music and savour all phases of the experience.

  Too many people say, "I would enjoy cooking if only I had the time." Well you always "have time", in this case 40 minutes of it! Delight in the process rather than waiting for the goal of the finished product. You'll taste the difference.
- I remember being taught this in home economics class at school and it even proved to be true! Bring out all the necessary ingredients and equipment before you start cooking. This streamlines preparation.
- If you discover at the last minute that you are missing an ingredient, don't panic. Familiarise yourself with the following chart and use your common sense. This is how creative new recipes are born.

LAST MINUTE EXCHANGES
FOR MISSING INGREDIENTS

What's missing:

- A major protein like the chicken someone ate for lunch which you had planned to cook in a sauce, stew, casserole, etc.

Some of your options:

- other meats, bacon, sausage, salami
- tinned fish
- avocado and nuts
- tinned beans
- hard-boiled eggs
- omelettes sliced into a stew or layered in a casserole
- noodles and seeds
- cubed cheese, tofu or tempeh
- cottage cheese or tofu bound with flour, egg and seasonings to make patties or dumplings
- starchy veg. like pumpkin, potato, kumara with nuts or seeds.

- A major carbohydrate like the noodles to your spaghetti dish or the potatoes to your scalloped potatoes.

- brown rice
- lentils or other legumes; tinned beans
- noodles
- high profile veg. like eggplant, pumpkin, potato, kumara
- garlic bread as a side dish

	• crumbled bread with sage, onion and egg to form croquettes or dumplings or as a layer in a casserole • long thinly sliced and steamed celery makes "green spaghetti" or use long thin strips of steamed carrot.
• Flour, being used as a binding agent as in patties, croquettes, savoury pie crusts, etc.	• bread crumbs, cracker crumbs • ground nuts or seeds • left-over cooked breakfast cereal • dry cereals like rice bubbles, rolled oats, wheatgerm, rice bran.
• Flour, as a thickener in sauces, stews, soups, etc. • Some crucial and flavourful ingredients to a sauce or sauce-component to a stew, casserole, soup etc, such as missing the tomatoes to a tomato sauce or lasagne	• arrowroot or cornflour • pureed cooked vegetables such as starchy veg., cauliflower, asparagus, broccoli. • be flexible! Change your tomato-less lasagne into an Indonesian Peanut Sauce casserole. Same concept, same vegetables, different flavourings. • always keep Vegetable Stock on hand in the fridge or freezer. This can be thickened and brought to the boil with 2 tbs rice flour per cup of stock and flavoured as follows: Provencal — 1 tsp basil, ½ tsp thyme, garlic, bay leaf, sardines or olives. Sweet and Sour — 2 tbs each: soy sauce, brown sugar, vinegar; 1 tsp each: coriander and Chinese 5-spice. Colonial Curry — use all or ½ coconut milk to replace stock, 1 tbs honey, 1 tsp each: peeled chopped ginger root, cumin, coriander; ½ tsp each: turmeric and nutmeg. Country Gravy — 1-2 tsp miso or marmite, 1 tbs food yeast, ½ tsp each: mixed herbs, paprika, garam masala, tarragon; ¼ tsp sage; minced onion. Italian — all stock or ½ diced tomatoes, 1 tbs each: vinegar and brown sugar, 1 tsp each: marmite, paprika, oreganum, basil; garlic, minced onion and capsicum. Indonesian Peanut — 3 tbs peanut butter, 1 tbs each: miso or marmite, lemon juice, honey, 1 tsp each: chopped peeled ginger root and cumin; ¼ tsp: turmeric and allspice.
• Eggs as a binding agent (rather than as a leavener such as in cakes or a souffle).	• mashed tofu • crumbled or grated cheese • 3 tbs Boiled Linseed to replace 1 egg.

DISASTERS
how to enjoy them and even eat them

Unless suffering from third-degree burns, most dishes can, when necessary, be refashioned into respectability. Presentation is always important and never more so when spooning what should have been a savoury loaf out of a "stuck" pan and into a gaily embellished casserole dish as the newly christened "Pate Greco".

Nothing is worse than to have the cook scuffle disconsolately — or flurry nervously — to the table and initiate the rites of dining with a list of apologies. Instead, adopt a Madonna-like smile, reassemble and exuberantly rechristen your creation and many is the time that it will elicit words of praise. Best of all the atmosphere of the table will not be disturbed, but enhanced.

A pressure cooker is not just the name for a type of saucepan, but can aptly describe the situation in one's kitchen, perhaps especially when cooking for guests. Use the steam that builds up to energetic and inspired advantage. One man's "failure" is another man's feast. A rose may be a rose may be a rose, but a fallen souffle can swiftly reincarnate as a successful "Persian Pancake". Following are some examples of what to do with mishaps, large and small.

First look at the impaired product; can something be done to rectify the difficulty or does it need complete restructuring?

Savoury loaf that sticks to the pan — if mostly salvageable pat into shape and top with cover-up sauce or garnish. If too wet but otherwise cooked, add rice bran or wheat germ or ground nuts to thicken, or, toss with steamed vegetables and serve out of a bowl.

If savoury loaf or patties are too dry and crumbly — mix with oil or Vegetable Stock or egg to bind, then repack into clean, oiled pan, rest in warm spot for 5-10 minutes and invert onto platter; or bind as above, then form into rissole or other small shape, roll in sesame seeds or ground nuts and briefly grill; or bind as above and press mixture into prepared pie plate or casserole dish as for a pie crust. Bake for 10 minutes in medium-high oven to crispen, then fill with steamed vegetables and sauce; serve.

Sauce or stew with an unpleasantly dominating flavour (e.g. too much of a particular herb) — add cumin powder, coriander or garam masala to overpower it; or add raw peeled potato to absorb flavour, cook, then discard potato.

Mayonnaise which separates — remove mixture from blender. Place egg and a dash of vinegar in blender as if starting a new batch, slowly drizzle in old batch as if it were the oil called for.

Cake which didn't rise — serve spread lavishly with fresh fruit and sauce; or cube and use in parfaits with fruit and dried fruit puree or sauce; or cool thoroughly, slice into thin layers and alternate with lemon or other filling, sauce, or frosting.

Edible cake "failures" — may be crumbled and used in making tortes.

Custard or fruit sauce too thin — add mashed banana, dried fruit puree, coconut, or ground nuts.

Baked custard that separates or stove-top custard that curdles — puree in blender as is or with fruit, spices, coconut, etc and serve as a sauce for fruit salad, desserts, breakfast.

Runny, unset pie filling — pour into tall glasses with alternate layers of crumbled pie crust mixed with coconut, nuts or fruit.

SPECIAL DIETS — everyone is on one!

Throughout this book there are numerous alternatives given to common staples and style of cooking. This is done for many reasons: for the benefit of those on Special Diets (diets which exclude certain foods such as wheat, gluten, milk, etc); for those interested in experimenting with new ideas and tastes; and importantly for those conscious of the dietary imbalances of our western culture evident in the unnatural predominance of certain foods. These include, among others: meat, milk products, eggs, wheat, gluten, sugar and salt. It is not that one should, categorically, avoid these foods but rather one can be aware of alternatives and make use of these as suitable.

Even if one experiences no marked, immediate repercussions to the intake of the above foods as would one who had a specific allergy or intolerance, because of their pervasive presence in our diets — sometimes over a few generations — an overriding influence has been extended which has coloured our entire eating pattern and thus way of life.

In a sense it is likenable to the situation of a person on mind-altering drugs who soon forgets what the nature of his undrugged state was. He begins to relate everything around him in terms of his now distorted state and gradually moves further and further astray from reality. No wonder many people find themselves needing to redress this imbalance through the medium of their own diet, thus acting as a rudder for a change in direction for society as a whole.

It is most freeing to move beyond the prescribed perimeter of cultural, familial and personal prejudice. Rather than becoming confined, horizons actually enlarge and the dietary alternatives are many. It is our vision which has been restrictive . . . not the range of alternatives. The process is truly one of expansion and renewal. Discernment replaces desire and there is a lightness to our living. A new ratio is often experienced: on less intake we know greater output.

Special Diets — everyone is rightly on one. It is for each of us to be discerning and specific in our living in all its particulars. It is this approach which enables healing in our own physical body and indeed for the body of mankind.

Some Particulars

It is important for those on Special Diets — if not everyone — to eat a variety of foods and not to depend heavily on any one food or range thereof. For instance, if one moves away from milk products to exchange this pattern for a hefty intake of soy products would still be to perpetuate an imbalance from which nutritional deficiencies result. If one already has a tendency to allergy, new intolerances can thus develop.

It has been said that there is no such thing as allergy (or any dis-ease for that matter) only a body — or a person — out of balance. Observing a particular diet is certainly important in the transition phase from so-called allergy to wellness. However the essential point is not mere maintenance, but renewal. The body is offering an explicit message that root change is called for.

NUTRITIONAL KNOW-HOW

Ideally we should receive all the necessary nutrients from our food. Unfortunately, even for those who stay away from processed and otherwise refined foods, our basic foods such as fruit, vegetables, grains and others, have also, sadly, been tampered with. Grown in deficient soils, weaned on chemical fertilisers and suffused with sprays, they may be only look-alike facsimiles of their intended selves. Following is an outline of vitamins and minerals and the foods they may (hopefully!) be found in. At times the discretionary use of organically based tablets and other supplements may be called for.

Remember that vitamins and minerals are sensitive to light and heat and are often water-soluble, so if improperly stored or cooked, nominally good foods will provide little nourishment. Check this list to see how varied your diet factually is, nutritionally speaking.

Vitamin	Food Source
A	red peppers, leafy greens, most meat, egg yolk, dried apricots, cod liver and halibut liver oil, sweet potatoes, carrot, tomatoes, orange juice and oil (in the peel), parsley.
B	food yeast, rice bran, grains, nuts, seeds, molasses, legumes, wheat germ, bean sprouts, potatoes, eggs.
C	citrus fruit, tomatoes, peppers, rosehips, parsley, black currants, acerola cherry, brussels sprouts, broccoli, cabbage, spinach, strawberries, potato, turnips, cabbage, onion.
D	halibut and cod liver oil, sea-fish, egg yolk, mushrooms, sunflower seeds, alfalfa.
E	whole wheat, green leafy vegetables, lettuce, watercress, oils; wheatgerm, soybean, corn and safflower; rice bran, nuts, seeds.
F	avocado, grains, seeds, green vegetables, lettuce.
K	kelp, alfalfa, leafy greens, egg yolks, molasses, yoghurt, safflower oil.

Mineral	Food Source
calcium	kelp, molasses, sesame seeds, carob, almonds, soybeans, food yeast, spinach, asparagus, potato skin, lemon, tomatoes, brazil nuts, milk products.
copper	mushrooms, peas, whole grains, leafy vegetables, seafoods, chicken.
iodine	pears, strawberries, seafood, kelp, potato skins, pineapple, broccoli, garlic, rhubarb.
iron	kelp, rice bran, food yeast, sesame seeds, egg, asparagus, cabbage, prunes, dates, blackberries, brown rice, beets.
magnesium	kelp, sunflower seeds, molasses, soybeans, nuts, buckwheat, peanuts, millet, lima beans, plums, coconut, figs, lettuce.
manganese	wheat and rice bran, walnuts, ginger, egg yolk, nasturtium leaves, rye flour, oatmeal, parsley, mint, chives.
phosphorous	pumpkin, raisins, barley, nuts, spinach, egg yolk, brown rice, brussels sprouts.
potassium	watermelon, kelp, molasses, food yeast, bananas, legumes, wheat, apricots, almonds, raisins, rye, parsley, potato and sweet potato, parsnip.
selenium	food yeast, garlic, liver, kidney, seafoods, dairy products, whole grains.
silicon	linseed, cucumber, oats, figs, pumpkin, asparagus, barley, parsnip, celery, brown rice, tomatoes, onion.

Stove-Top Menus

SOUPS

1	*Sophisticate Soup*	*SERVES 4*

- *Cream of Cauliflower and Ginger Soup* •
- *Toasted Almond Topping* •
- *Cracker Selection* •

This is a Grande Dame of soups: smooth and subtly exotic. Accompany with a crunchy and colourful nut and vegetable topping and a simple array of crackers.

Preparation Plan
- prepare soup
- prepare topping
- arrange crackers, and serve

Cream of Cauliflower and Ginger Soup

½ medium cauliflower
1½ cups chopped kumara
1 small-medium onion
10mm peeled ginger, chopped
2-3 cloves garlic
3 cups water or Vegetable Stock

1½ cups coconut cream
2 sticks celery, angle-sliced
1½ tsp garam masala
¼ tsp thyme
¼ tsp nutmeg
herb salt

Bring all the vegetables (except celery) to the boil with the ginger, garlic and water or stock. Then simmer briskly for 10 minutes, or longer, until the vegetables are tender.

Allow to cool, then in several batches whizz soup in a blender with portions of the coconut cream until all is pureed. Return to the saucepan and add the remaining ingredients. Bring back to the boil and simmer for 5 minutes or longer. Taste for seasoning.

Toasted Almond Topping

½ cup almonds
1 small red pepper, cubed
½ cup mung bean sprouts

1 tbs cold-pressed oil
1 tsp coriander

Coarsely chop the almonds, and toast them. Toss with the remaining ingredients.

Cracker Selection

Kai-Ora rice crackers
Healtheries rice crackers

Vitalia gluten-free sourdough breads
Vi-tal margarine or butter

Arrange a selection of your favourite breads or crackers and serve with margarine, butter, garlic butter or cream cheese.

Southern Hospitality

• *Creole Gumbo — Vegetable or Seafood* •
• *Cornbread Wedges* •
• *Avocado Platter* •

The beckoning invitation of homemade soup, especially when in the company of bread hot from the oven. The soup can be further flavoured and garnished with the addition of a swirl of yoghurt or sour cream, crumbled bacon or blue vein cheese, or grilled cubes of tofu sprinkled with soy sauce.

Preparation Plan
- prepare soup; preheat oven
- prepare and bake bread
- prepare salad platter, and serve

Creole Gumbo

6 large spinach leaves, chopped	2 large potatoes, cubed or ⅔ cup macaroni
1½ cups chopped tomatoes	4 spring onions, chopped
handful parsley	3 bay leaves
3 cloves garlic	2 tsp paprika
2 cups milk (soy, goat, cow, coconut cream)	1 tsp basil
3 cups Vegetable Stock	½ tsp thyme
or part white wine	cayenne and herb salt to taste
1 tbs lemon juice	option: add mussels, chunks of fish,
4 tbs rice flour or other	squid rings

Whizz spinach, tomatoes, parsley, garlic and some of the liquid in a blender. Pour it into the soup pot and add remaining ingredients. Add seafood option if desired. Bring to the boil and simmer for 30 minutes or more. Taste for seasoning.

While soup is coming to the boil, preheat oven to 220ºC and prepare the Cornbread.

Cornbread Wedges

1 cup cornmeal	1 cup milk
1 cup rice flour or other	¼ cup cold-pressed oil
2 tbs honey	1 egg
3 tsp baking powder or	½-1 tsp herb salt
1 tbs Prepared Yeast	1 cup kernel corn (optional)

Beat all the ingredients vigorously for one minute. Pour into·a greased 25cm frypan. Bake for 20 minutes until centre springs back when lightly touched. Serve directly from the frypan.

Avocado Platter

1-2 large ripe avocados	alfalfa sprouts
1 large red pepper	paprika

Place a mound of alfalfa sprouts at the centre of your serving platter. Surround with slices of avocado and red pepper. Sprinkle avocado with paprika.

3 Sweet Lentil or Noodle Soup *SERVES 4*

• Sweet Lentil or Noodle Soup •
• Tahini Topping •
• Popcorn USA •

Soup with a Middle Eastern flair and topped with a creamy swirl of yoghurt or tofu whip mixed with tahini. Tahini is a sesame seed paste available from delicatessens and health food stores. It adds a delicious flavour to dressings, sauces and sandwiches. Do try the popcorn; served hot and fresh it is crunchy and more-ish. Make lots, for it keeps well as a snack for later.

Preparation Plan
- prepare soup
- prepare topping
- prepare popcorn, and serve

Sweet Lentil or Noodle Soup

4 cups water	3 tbs miso or marmite
¾ cup red lentils	2 tbs tahini
or 1 cup small noodles	2 tbs peanut butter
2 large carrots, diced	2 tbs honey
1 cup broccoli pieces	1 tbs cumin powder
1 cup chopped green beans	½ tsp turmeric

Place all the ingredients in a large pot and bring to the boil, partly covered (lentils tend to foam). Simmer for 30 minutes or more until the lentils are tender. Taste for seasoning.

Tahini Topping

¾ cup yoghurt or Savoury Tofu Whip	4 tbs tahini
or mayonnaise	

Combine both ingredients until smooth. Once soup is in bowls, swirl a spiral of the mixture onto each bowl.

Popcorn USA

¼ cup popping corn	oil or melted butter or margarine
2 tbs oil	herb salt or food yeast or grated parmesan

Place the 2 tablespoons oil in an electric frypan or cast-iron pan with a lid. Turn heat to high and let the oil heat until almost smoking. Add the popping corn, immediately cover and shake pan to coat corn with oil. Continue shaking regularly and cook for 5 minutes or more, keeping heat as high as possible, until all popping sound has ceased. Do not lift lid until this point.

Pour into a large bowl and toss with oil or margarine or butter and choice of seasoning.

---

4   *Red Russian Borsch*

- *Red Russian Borsch* •
- *Sourdough Bread or Rice Crackers* •
- *Gouda or Goat's Milk Camembert* •

Do try to get fresh dill for the soup — a traditional and sublimely flavourful touch. There are many types of borsch and not all of them contain beets, but whatever the base it ranks high on the list of satisfying soups. This is full of vegetables but, if you wish to add something raw and complementary, try cucumber slices marinated in vinegar and salt.

Preparation Plan
- prepare soup
- set out bread and cheese, and serve

Red Russian Borsch

2½-3 cups chopped beets
3 cups chopped cabbage
1½ cups chopped potato
½ cup chopped onion
½ cup chopped tomatoes
2 tsp paprika
2-4 cloves garlic, chopped
¼ tsp turmeric
¼ tsp allspice
3 tbs oil

4 cups water
2 tbs honey
2 tbs apple cider vinegar
2 tbs miso or marmite
3 bay leaves
4 tbs fresh dill or
    1½ tsp dill seed
2 tsp basil

Fry the vegetables and spices in oil until tender. Add the remaining ingredients and bring to the boil. Simmer for 20 minutes or more. Taste for seasoning.

Bread and Cheese

hearty sourdough rye
round and rectangular rice crackers
salad vegetables

gouda or Saint Paulin or
    sheep's milk feta or
    goat's milk camembert

Set out an attractive selection of breads, crackers and cheese. May be served with radishes, gherkins and vinegared cucumber slices.

- *Eyeball Soup* •
- *Antipasto* •

You will read this recipe if just to find out what the title really refers to. This is a type of soup popular in Italy, Spain and Portugal — where it is named more romantically — and is really a variation of egg on toast. A flavourful stock is poured into soup bowls filled with garlic toast, a poached egg, and a sprinkle of cheese. Wonderful peasant fare. Accompany with an antipasto served as finger food.

Preparation Plan

- prepare soup
- prepare antipasto, and serve

Eyeball Soup

4 cups chicken or Vegetable Stock
4 tbs food yeast
1-2 tsp curry powder
1 tsp bouquet garni
½ tsp sage
½ tsp nutmeg
herb salt or miso or marmite

4 thick slices bread, such as
   gluten-free cornbread
butter or margarine
lots of garlic!
4 large eggs
parmesan or sheep's milk feta

Bring the stock to the boil with the seasonings. Turn to low and simmer for 10 minutes or more. Taste for seasonings.

Grill bread on one side until crisp. Turn to the other side and spread with a mixture of the butter and garlic. Grill.

Poach the eggs. Place one slice of toast in each soup bowl. Top with an egg and sprinkle with ample cheese. Pour stock on top and serve immediately.

Antipasto

Dressing:
4 tbs olive oil
1 tbs lemon juice
1 tsp prepared mustard
1 tsp basil
herb salt to taste

lettuce leaves
carrot sticks
cauliflower segments
celery sticks
sliced mushrooms
freshly ground black pepper

Combine all dressing ingredients and taste for seasoning.

On a large platter arrange a bed of lettuce leaves. Top with a selection of raw vegetables and any other options. Drizzle generously with the dressing and sprinkle with freshly ground black pepper.

The platter may also be accompanied with a mixture of Homemade Mayonnaise and chopped garlic.

- *Swedish Spinach Soup* •
- *Choice of Garnish* •
- *Crunchy Veg. and Crackers* •

The satisfaction of soup. This one is green, creamy and rich-tasting, yet light in fact. Garnish traditionally with chopped hard-boiled egg; thematically with pickled herring; or experimentally with one of the other tasty garnishes.

Preparation Plan
- prepare soup
- prepare garnish
- set out veg. and crackers, and serve

Swedish Spinach Soup

6 cups chicken or Vegetable Stock
800g spinach, well chopped
3 large potatoes, quartered
2 tsp basil
2 tsp oreganum
1 tsp bouquet garni

½ tsp nutmeg
2-4 cloves garlic, chopped
herb salt
2 cups milk (soy, goat, cow, coconut cream)

Bring all the ingredients — except the milk — to the boil, then turn to simmer for 5 minutes. Turn off heat and remove spinach and potatoes to a blender. Add milk and whizz. Return to the pot and simmer for 20 minutes or longer until thick and flavourful. Pour into soup bowls; garnish and serve.

Garnish

options:
   garlic croutons
   cubed tofu or tempeh

chopped hard-boiled eggs
cooked bacon or ham or salami
pickled herring

Select option and use to garnish the soup. To make garlic croutons spread thick slices of bread with garlic butter. Slice into small squares and fry until crisp.

Crunchy Veg. and Crackers

raw cauliflower segments
carrot sticks

cucumber sticks
rice crackers or other

Attractively arrange a selection of raw vegetables and crackers or bread.

Summer Soup

- *Summer Soup* •
- *Vegetable Platter* •
- *Corn Chips or Pita Bread* •

So called because of its avocado content, Summer Soup is delicious hot or cold or served in small portions as an elegant first course. For those who like it hot, trace a spiral of hot chilli sauce on each bowlful. Serve with crisp chips and raw vegetables. For hearty diners add sliced chicken or squid rings to the soup, or serve cheese wedges on the vegetable platter.

Preparation Plan
- prepare soup
- prepare vegetable platter
- set out chips, and serve

Summer Soup

2 large ripe avocados	¼ cup dry sherry
1¾ cups cream or coconut cream	2 tsp basil
4 cups chicken stock or	½ tsp nutmeg
flavourful Vegetable Stock	herb salt

In a blender puree the avocado with the cream. Bring the stock to the boil, then turn to low. Whisk in the avocado, sherry and seasonings. Taste and serve, or chill and serve cold.

Garnish as above or with additional sliced avocado.

Vegetable Platter

carrot sticks	tomato wedges
courgette sticks	cheese fingers (optional)

Arrange on a platter and serve.

Chips or Bread
corn chips or pita bread or bread sticks

Arrange in a basket and serve.

8   *Spas* SERVES 4

- *Yoghurt and Barley (or Buckwheat) Soup* •
  - *Black Bread and Caviar* •
  - *Stix* •

"Spas" is a soup which originates in the Caucasus region of Russia, where it is served hot or cold. It is traditionally accompanied with black bread and caviar or thin strips of pickled herring. Caviar can be purchased at any large supermarket and ranges in price from very cheap to gulpingly expensive.

Preparation Plan
- cook barley and prepare soup
- set out bread and toppings
- prepare vegetables, and serve

Spas

½ cup pearl barley or buckwheat	2 tbs butter or margarine
3 cups water or Vegetable Stock	3 tbs finely chopped fresh mint
4 eggs	1 tbs coriander
3 tbs rice flour or other	1 tsp or more herb salt
2 cups plain yoghurt or coconut cream	extra chopped fresh mint and parsley
¼ cup finely chopped onions	lemon slices

In a medium saucepan bring the barley and 2 cups water to the boil. Boil uncovered for 30 minutes (15 minutes for buckwheat) or longer while preparing remaining ingredients.

In a large saucepan thoroughly beat the eggs. Whisk in the flour a tablespoon at a time, then whisk in the yoghurt or coconut cream and one cup water. Over a high heat bring almost to the boil (at no point let it boil or it will curdle), whisking constantly.

Turn heat to low and simmer for 5 minutes until slightly thickened. Stir in the barley and its water, and the onion, butter, mint, coriander and salt. Simmer for 5-10 minutes over a low heat and taste for seasoning. Pour into bowls and garnish with mint, parsley and lemon.

Black Bread and Caviar

hearty sourdough breads such as Vitalia brand	butter or margarine
	caviar or pickled herring

Arrange attractively and serve.

Stix

whole radishes	cucumber sticks
gherkins	carrot sticks

Arrange attractively and serve.

9 *Garlic & Tomato Stew*   SERVES 4-5

• *Garlic and Tomato Stew with Fish or Tofu* •
• *Mashed Potatoes* •
• *Cabbage Salad* •

Good peasanty fare. With all the garlic not heavy-date material but enjoyable in other ways.

Preparation Plan
- prepare salad, cover and chill
- steam potatoes; mash while preparing fish or tofu
- prepare fish or tofu, and serve

Cabbage Salad

2 tbs lemon juice	1 tsp paprika
1 tsp grated lemon peel	grated cabbage
1 cup Homemade Mayonnaise or yoghurt	finely chopped, peeled cucumber

Combine all the ingredients except the vegetables, then stir in the vegetables. Cover and chill until serving time.

Mashed Potatoes

potatoes

Chop potatoes into small pieces. Steam for 5-10 minutes until tender. Mash and blend in some of the hot potato liquid until fluffy and of desired consistency.

Garlic and Tomato Stew with Fish or Tofu

olive oil	herb salt
1 large onion, sliced	4 fish steaks or 2 blocks tofu
2 tsp finely chopped garlic	sliced in half horizontally
3 large tomatoes, chopped	2 tbs chopped parsley
1-2 tsp mild curry powder	

In olive oil cook the onion and garlic until tender, but not brown. Stir in the tomatoes and seasonings and cook for 5-10 minutes until thick and well coloured. Add fish or tofu and parsley and simmer for 10-15 minutes until tender and flavourful.

- *Stewed Red Lentils in Barbecue Sauce* •
- *Toasted Wholemeal Buns or Cornbread* •
- *Green Garden Platter* •

Simple enough for summertime, nourishing enough for a winter's meal — and a good idea for vegetarian guests at a barbecue. The stew is great served right on top of split toasted buns. The salad can be eaten on the side or used as further sandwich material for a messy mile-high creation. If you prefer to use red kidney or other beans which require soaking, refer to the quick-cooking bean method in the Cook's Tips section.

Preparation Plan
- cook lentils; prepare sauce and mix with lentils
- prepare salad platter
- toast buns or bread, and serve

Stewed Red Lentils in Barbecue Sauce

1¼ cups red lentils

Place the lentils in a medium to large saucepan with ample water. Bring to the boil with the lid only partly covering (all legumes foam). Boil vigorously for 10 minutes or longer while preparing sauce.

Barbecue Sauce:

cold-pressed oil	3 tbs brown sugar
5-6 medium tomatoes, chopped	3 tbs natural soy sauce
1 green pepper, sliced	2 tbs prepared mustard
1 large onion, sliced	dash cayenne
lots of garlic!	rice flour or other
3 tbs apple cider vinegar	Vegetable Stock

Fry the vegetables in oil over a brisk heat until tender. Add the remaining ingredients and bring to the boil.

Meanwhile drain the lentils of excess water and add them to the sauce. Once a vigorous boil has been reached, turn the heat to low and simmer for 20 minutes or longer until the lentils are soft and tender and the stew is flavourful. To thicken or thin, whisk in rice flour or Vegetable Stock.

Green Garden Platter

shredded lettuce	celery sticks
gherkins, sliced	lemon juice
avocado slices	

On an oval platter place sections of individual vegetables to create a striped effect. Drizzle avocado with lemon juice.

Toasted Wholemeal Buns or Cornbread

wholemeal buns or (gluten-free) cornbread or see recipe for Cornbread Wedges

Split buns or slice bread and toast just before serving.

---

11   *Sweet Potato Stew*   *SERVES 4*

• *Cucumber and Sweet Potato Stew* •
• *Brazil Nut Topping* •
• *Avocado Slices* •

Preparation Plan
- bring stew to the boil and simmer until tender
- toast nuts
- slice avocado, and serve

Cucumber and Sweet Potato Stew

3 medium cucumber (about 1kg),
   peeled, seeded, and finely chopped
4 medium sweet potatoes
250g green beans, sliced
½ cup chopped spring onions
3 gherkins, diced

3 tbs chopped fresh mint
3 tbs chopped parsley
1 cup chicken or Vegetable Stock
1 cup milk (cow, goat, soy, coconut cream)
1 tsp finely chopped ginger root
herb salt

Bring all the ingredients to the boil and simmer for 20 - 30 minutes. Taste for seasoning. Sprinkle in rice flour to thicken if necessary. Serve sprinkled with Brazil Nut Topping.

Brazil Nut Topping

2 tbs cold-pressed oil
¾ cup coarsely chopped brazil nuts

½ cup cracker or dry bread crumbs
1 tsp cumin powder

Over a medium heat toast the nuts in the oil for about 3 minutes, until medium-brown. Stir in the crumbs and cumin powder and continue to toast until golden brown.

Avocado Slices

1-2 avocados

Peel and slice the avocado, and serve.

Minestrone Stew

- *Minestrone Stew* •
- *Noodle Dumplings* •
- *Pepper Strips* •

A thicker stew version of the classic Italian minestrone soup. Here it is served with light noodle dumplings, with the simple succulence of sweet red pepper as an accompaniment.

Preparation Plan
- prepare soup
- prepare dumplings and steam-cook on stew
- slice pepper, and serve

Minestrone Stew

5 cups Vegetable Stock or water
2 cups chopped tomatoes
4-5 cups mixed vegetables such as: leek,
  carrot, onion, courgette, broccoli, peas
chopped parsley
3 tbs rice flour or other
3 tbs apple cider vinegar

2 tbs honey or brown sugar
2 tbs miso or marmite
3 bay leaves
1 tbs basil
2-4 cloves garlic, chopped
1 tsp mixed herbs
herb salt

Bring all the ingredients to the boil, then simmer for 20 minutes or longer. The stew will thicken further with the addition of the noodles.

Noodle Dumplings

200g rice or wheat vermicelli noodles
3 eggs
1½ cups rice flour or other
¼ cup milk (goat, soy, cow, coconut cream)
1 tbs baking powder or
 1 tbs Prepared Yeast

3 tbs cold-pressed oil
2 tsp oreganum
½ tsp sage
½ tsp nutmeg
1-2 tsp herb salt
paprika

When the soup has been turned to simmer, add the noodles breaking half of them into small pieces. Leave the remainder whole and submerge them as a mass without stirring them throughout the stew. Simmer for 5 minutes, then with slotted spoon lift out as many of the long noodles as is easily possible. Drain off their excess liquid. Roughly chop the noodles to about 15mm lengths.

Thoroughly beat the eggs, then beat in the remaining ingredients including the chopped noodles (about one cup). Spoon large tablespoon amounts onto the simmering stew. Cover with a lid and steam-cook undisturbed for 12 minutes. Sprinkle with paprika and serve.

Pepper Strips

2 red peppers

Slice in long strips and serve.

- *Fish or Tofu with Almond Tamarillo Sauce* •
- *Speckled Noodles* •
- *Cucumber Fingers* •

A variation of the Garlic and Tomato Stew recipe. Chicken, veal or other quick-cooking meat could be used in either recipe, as could squid, mussels and other seafood. The hot noodles are tossed with raw vegetables as a kind of salad. Steamed potato or another starchy vegetable can be used in place of the noodles.

Preparation Plan
- prepare sauce, and cook fish or tofu in it
- cook noodles; toss with vegetables
- slice cucumber, and serve

Fish or Tofu with Almond Tamarillo Sauce

½ cup almonds	1 tsp paprika
1 cup orange juice	1 tsp diced ginger root
4 tamarillos, peeled and chopped	½ tsp mixed herbs
2 medium carrots, diced	whole, gutted and scaled fish
2 tbs miso or marmite	or fish steaks
1 tsp brown sugar	or 2 blocks tofu, cubed or sliced

Toast the almonds. Grind half of them and coarsely chop the rest. Set aside.

In an electric frypan or other large-based pan bring to the boil the remaining ingredients (except fish or tofu). Turn to simmer and cook gently for 10 minutes.

Stir in ground almonds, adding more nuts or more juice to adjust thickening. Add fish steaks or tofu and cook gently for 10 minutes. Cook the whole fish for 10-12 minutes on each side. Sprinkle with chopped almonds and serve.

Speckled Noodles

rice-noodles or other	3 tbs cold-pressed oil
½ cup chopped silverbeet or spinach	1 tsp basil
½ cup sliced mushrooms	1 tsp oreganum
3 tbs chopped parsley	herb salt

Cook noodles according to packet directions. For rice-flour noodles, bring water to the boil, add the noodles, cover, turn off heat and let sit for 8 minutes.

Toss hot, drained noodles with remaining ingredients.

Cucumber Fingers

cucumber

Peel cucumber, slice in half, and slice each section into lengths or fingers. Serve in a small glass bowl or pitcher.

14   *Bombay Coconut Curry*   Serves 4

• *Bombay Coconut Curry* •
• *Mint and Cumin Lima Beans* •
• *Carrot Salad* •

The curry can be as mild or as hot as you choose. The protein comes from the combination of coconut milk and beans but for heartier appetites cubes of lamb steak, chicken breast or liver, fish, squid, tofu or tempeh, or boiled eggs may be added in with the vegetables and likewise cooked.

Preparation Plan
- prepare lima beans
- cook curry
- prepare salad, and serve

Mint and Cumin Lima Beans

1½ cups lima beans	1-2 tbs food yeast to taste
3 tbs cold-pressed oil	1 tbs honey
3 tbs chopped fresh mint	2 tsp cumin powder
1 tbs lemon juice	herb salt to taste

Boil the beans, with ample water to cover, until tender, for about 20 minutes (no soaking necessary with limas). Drain and toss with the remaining ingredients. Keep warm until ready to serve.

Bombay Coconut Curry

kumara chunks	1-2 tbs mild curry powder
cauliflower chunks	2 tsp coriander
peas or green beans	1 tsp chopped peeled ginger root
brussels sprouts, halved	½ tsp turmeric
or other seasonal vegetables	herb salt to taste
1 tin coconut cream	coconut
¼ cup or more Vegetable Stock	

Combine all the ingredients except coconut in a large pot. Bring to the boil and simmer for 15 minutes or more until tender. Add more vegetable stock to thin if necessary. Place in a serving bowl and sprinkle with coconut.

Carrot Salad

carrots	yoghurt (optional)
lettuce or silverbeet	

On a serving plate or in a shallow bowl arrange a mound of grated carrot surrounded by shredded lettuce or silverbeet. Place a sprig of fresh mint at the centre and drizzle yoghurt decoratively over the carrot.

---

15 Pumpkin & Tamarillo Stew *SERVES 4*

• Pumpkin and Tamarillo Stew •
• Puffs •
• Radish Jacks •

Little can surpass the rich aroma and impending pleasure of a homey stew. Chunks of nourishing and inexpensive sheep's heart or kidneys may be added or other quick-cooking meat. This stew is served with the pleasing crunch of toasted unsweetened puffed cereal (see Glossary) and a whimsically presented raw vegetable.

Preparation Plan
- bring stew ingredients to the boil, and simmer until tender
- toast puffed cereal
- slice and arrange radishes, and serve

Pumpkin and Tamarillo Stew

2 cups water or Vegetable Stock	2 tbs molasses
3 cups cubed pumpkin	1 tsp chopped ginger root
1½ cups cauliflower	1 tsp chopped garlic
1 cup sliced cabbage	8cm stick cinnamon
1 cup peeled, cubed tamarillo	2 whole cloves
½ cup sliced green beans	2 bay leaves
2 medium onions, sliced	½ tsp bouquet garni
3 tbs peanut butter	
3 tbs miso or marmite	rice flour to thicken

Bring all the ingredients to the boil (including optional meat as above). Simmer for 30 minutes until tender. Taste for seasoning; remove bay leaves, cloves and cinnamon. Sprinkle in rice flour and simmer until bubbly and thickened to desired consistency.

Puffs
1 cup puffed corn (such as Blackmores brand)

Toast puffed corn in a sturdy pan over a low-medium heat until lightly browned and crisp. Serve in a small bowl, plain or seasoned with salt, soy sauce or spices like cumin.

Radish Jacks
radishes

Slice radishes into 3mm slices. Slice each one to half its diameter.

Place 2 slices at right angles to each other and join at cuts.

• *Brasado al Marsala with Tofu or Fish or Meat* •
• *Crisp Salad* •

Italian for "braised in Marsala" this menu features a one-step, one-pot dish of braised protein option, vegetables and sauce. Marsala is my favourite sweet cooking wine, and this menu is a favourite quickie when I'm just cooking for myself. Any number of vegetables may be cooked in the pot so the only needed accompaniment is something raw and crisp.

Preparation Plan
- prepare one-pot dish
- prepare salad, and serve

Brasado al Marsala

protein option:
2-3 blocks tofu in thick slices
fish steaks or fillets and/or
   squid and mussels
pork chops or steaks
chicken pieces
kumara, halved or quartered

small cauliflower segments
onion, sliced
whole baby mushrooms
½-1 cup white wine
3 tbs natural soy sauce
3 tbs Marsala

Lightly oil a large frypan or electric frypan. If using chicken or pork brown the meat briefly on both sides.

With the meat, fish or tofu in the pan, surround and cover with the vegetables — make sure the larger or longer-cooking vegetables are on the bottom for faster cooking.

Cover with the wines and soy sauce. Use the lesser amount of wine with the tofu or fish as the briefer cooking time means less evaporates. Cover with a lid. Bring to the boil and immediately turn to simmer. Gently simmer tofu or fish for 15 minutes. Simmer pork or chicken for 20-30 minutes until tender.

Crisp Salad

lettuce or bean sprouts
thin carrot slices
angle-cut celery slices
olive oil

lemon juice
curry powder
chopped chives

Arrange salad on a platter. Drizzle with oil and lemon juice. Sprinkle with chives and curry powder.

17 *Hungarian Goulash* SERVES 4-5

• *Hungarian Goulash with Tofu or Chicken or Veal* •
• *Lemon Potatoes* •
• *Carraway Salad* •

Many are the variations on goulash. Despite the marauding Eastern invaders of their history, stews in the Austro-Hungarian Empire would have been as likely to include a block of tofu as a block of wood. But let us not quibble about authenticity when ease and flavour are present! Lard — pork or bacon fat — is traditionally used in preparing foods from this locale as it distinctively colours and flavours the paprika and onions which are foundational to many dishes.

Preparation Plan
• prepare goulash
• prepare potatoes
• prepare salad, and serve

Hungarian Goulash

3 tbs lard or butter or oil
1 cup finely chopped onions
2 tbs paprika
1 tsp finely chopped garlic
2-3 blocks tofu, cubed
   or 3 chicken breasts, sliced
   or 700g veal, sliced

1 cup chicken or Vegetable Stock
herb salt
4 tbs rice flour or other
2 cups sour cream or yoghurt
   or coconut cream

Slowly and evenly fry the onions, paprika and garlic in the lard until tender. Briefly fry the tofu or meat.

Add the stock and salt and bring to the boil. Reduce the heat to low and simmer for 20 minutes.

Meanwhile whisk the flour with the cream, stir into the goulash and simmer for 5-10 minutes over a low heat (do not boil), until thick and smooth.

Lemon Potatoes

very small whole potatoes
1 lemon, grated

lemon juice

Steam the potatoes until tender. Toss with the lemon juice and grated rind.

Carraway Salad

Dressing:
3 tbs cold-pressed oil
2 tbs white wine vinegar
½ tsp carraway seeds
salt and pepper

lettuce
tomato
cucumber
green pepper

Combine all the dressing ingredients, then toss with the vegetables and serve.

- *Stroganoff with Tempeh or Chicken or Beef or Fish Steaks* •
  - *Noodles or Steamed Kumara (Sweet Potato)* •
- *Crunchy Cucumber Salad with Tahini Mustard Dressing* •

Stroganoff is a simple dish of Russian origin which has had some tasty alterations in its movement west. The flavourful creamy sauce with protein option (traditionally beef) is scrumptious on noodles or a starchy vegetable like kumara.

Preparation Plan
- prepare stroganoff
- cook noodles or kumara
- prepare salad and dressing, and serve

Stroganoff

4 tbs oil or preferably butter
  or chicken or bacon fat
2 large onions, sliced not chopped
3 cloves garlic, chopped
2 sticks celery, chopped
2 courgettes or
  few green beans, diced
1 cup sliced mushrooms

one of the following protein options:
  ¾-1 block tempeh, cubed
  ½ kg beef fillet, in small thin slices

2 chicken breasts, sliced
2-4 fish steaks in medium-large segments

1 tbs paprika
1½ cups cream or coconut cream
½ cup tomato puree
½ cup white wine or Vegetable Stock
1 tsp oreganum
¾ tsp thyme
½ tsp nutmeg
¼ tsp allspice
herb salt

Over a low slow heat fry the vegetables in oil (or option) until tender, for about 10 minutes. Fry in one of the protein options until lightly cooked. Stir in paprika and cook for 2-3 minutes. Add remaining ingredients and bring to the boil. Simmer for 15-20 minutes until thick and richly flavourful.

Noodles or Steamed Kumara (Sweet Potato)
ribbon-shaped or other noodles — wheat or rice-flour based
  or kumara, sliced

Cook noodles according to packet instructions. For rice noodles: bring ample water to the boil, add noodles, cover, turn off heat and let sit for 8 minutes. Drain.

Or steam kumara for 5-8 minutes, until tender.

Crunchy Cucumber Salad with Tahini Mustard Dressing
Tahini Mustard Dressing:
½ cup Homemade Mayonnaise
3 tbs tahini or peanut butter
3 tbs Vegetable Stock or pineapple juice

1 tbs natural soy sauce
2 tsp prepared mustard
1 tsp honey

Blend together Mayonnaise and tahini or option. Then blend in the remaining ingredients.

Crunchy Cucumber Salad:
cucumber, peeled and sliced
lettuce in chunks

mung bean sprouts
poppy seeds

On a large platter toss the vegetables. Drape with Dressing, sprinkle with poppy seeds and serve.

19   *Chef's Summer Salad*   SERVES 4

- *Chef's Summer Salad with many variations* •
- *Choice of Dressings and Sauces* •
- *Corn on the Cob (optional)* •

A couldn't-be-simpler dinner ever popular with hot summertime cooks, and one with enough yummy ingredients to please varied individual tastes. For more bulk this meal is excellent with corn on the cob but the salad is still substantial on its own. Serve accompanied by one or more dressings·or sauces. Always make your dressings in generous quantity so that there is extra for other uses.

Preparation Plan
- cook potato or pasta and toss salad
- steam corn
- prepare one or more dressings or sauces, and serve

Chef's Summer Salad

4-6 large potatoes or equivalent
   pumpkin, kumara or pasta
2 avocados, in chunks
lettuce leaves, broken
carrots, thinly sliced
mushrooms, sliced
tomatoes, quartered
	protein options:
	   grilled or fried tofu or tempeh
	   hard-boiled eggs or strips of omelette
	   crumbled feta or grated cheese
	   tinned or freshly cooked fish
	   salami, ham, bacon or
	     left-over cooked meat

Chop potato (or kumara or pumpkin) into small chunks and steam; or if using pasta, cook and drain.

Place potato or option in a large bowl to toss with remaining ingredients and one or more of the protein options. Or keep the salad all-vegetable and serve with a hearty sauce like Peanut Sauce and sprinkle with additional toasted peanuts. Serve salad on a large platter.

Corn on the Cob
corn on the cob

Steam corn for 10-15 minutes until a kernel is easily and juicily pierced by a fork.

Dressings and Sauces

Homemade Mayonnaise Mint Mayonnaise or Yoghurt Texas Barbecue Sauce	Chinese 5-Dragon Sauce Savoury Tofu Whip Mexicali Sauce Peanut Sauce

Choose one or more of those listed. Sauces may be served hot, room temperature or cold.

- *Tomato Flowers in Full Bloom* •
- *Tangy Lemon Dressing* •
- *Rye Toast Triangles or Rice Crackers* •

The attractiveness of this presentation is especially welcome to jaded hot-weather appetites, and ably suits a special luncheon. Here large tomatoes are sliced into sixths, leaving the base intact so the tomato will open into six petals. The tomatoes are generously filled with a moist flavourful split pea salad and served on a bed of spinach leaves. Of course numerous hot or cold, rice, potato, pasta or other combinations could serve as harmoniously.

Preparation Plan
- cook split peas; prepare filling and tomatoes
- prepare dressing
- prepare toast, and serve

Tomatoes in Full Bloom

1¼ cups yellow or green split peas (or options as above)	¼ cup currants
	6 olives, chopped
	3 tbs sesame seeds
1 cup or more peeled, cubed telegraph cucumber	2 tbs olive oil
	herb salt
2 sticks celery, diced	4 large tomatoes

Bring peas to the boil with ample water in a medium-large saucepan with lid only partly covering (all legumes foam). Boil vigorously for 30 minutes or until tender. Drain.

Meanwhile prepare filling. Toast sesame seeds and combine with remaining ingredients. Stir in drained split peas and taste for seasoning. Remember that the dressing will add further piquancy.

Slice tomatoes as above. Serve any remaining filling on the side.

Lemon Dressing

½ cup cold-pressed oil	1 tsp tarragon
4 tbs lemon juice	1 tsp dried mint
1 tbs food yeast	¼ tsp turmeric
2 tsp honey	herb salt
1½ tsp grated lemon peel	

Place all the ingredients in a small jar, cover, and shake to combine. Taste for seasoning.

Use some dressing to drizzle over each filled tomato and pass remainder.

Rye Toast Triangles or Rice Crackers

hearty plain or sourdough rye bread or rice crackers	margarine, butter or garlic butter

Toast bread and slice into triangles. Serve with plain or garlic butter.

- *Lentil Salad* •
- *Red, White and Blue Dressing* •
- *Spokes* •

This salad is yummy hot or cold. If serving cold give it as much chilling time as possible — if you have the time cook the lentils on the previous day to achieve this. Of course it can also be served with bread, sliced avocado or cheese for heartier appetites.

Preparation Plan
- cook lentils and prepare salad
- prepare dressing
- prepare vegetable spokes, and serve

Lentil Salad

1 cup lentils	2 tbs red wine vinegar
½ cup finely chopped red onions	2 tbs natural soy sauce
2 tbs chopped parsley	4 tbs olive oil
½ tsp finely chopped garlic	

Pour the lentils into ample rapidly boiling water. Turn heat to low and cook partly covered (watch for foaming) for 20 minutes until tender. Drain thoroughly and toss with remaining ingredients. Cover and chill as long as possible.

Red, White and Blue Dressing

1 medium tomato	¼ cup olive oil
¼ cup blue cheese or feta	1 tsp paprika
or hard-boiled eggs	herb salt
or toasted nuts or seeds	dash cayenne

In a blender whizz all the ingredients until thick and smooth. Serve as an accompaniment to the lentil salad and the spokes.

Spokes

carrots	mushrooms
courgettes	crackers or corn chips or
red pepper	crisp toast fingers

Arrange chips or option, spears and slices of vegetables as spokes on a round platter. Use the Dressing as a hub at the centre.

22 *Louis Pappas' Greek Salad* SERVES 4-6

• Louis Pappas' Greek Salad •
• Wine Dressings •

Of the many possible chef salad variations, this is one of renown, originating at the Louis Pappas' Cafe in Florida. Based on the classic Greek salad of lettuce, feta cheese and olives, it is a luscious montage of Greek foods and foreign adaptations. As a cold weather option serve the potato hot. Pita bread could accompany it but the salad is substantial.

Preparation Plan
- cook potatoes
- prepare dressings; toss, and serve

Louis Pappas' Greek Salad and Wine Dressings

Salad:
8-12 small potatoes
1 medium red onion, finely chopped
¼ cup parsley, chopped

Red Wine Dressing:
6 tbs red wine vinegar
1 cup olive oil
1 tsp paprika
1 tsp or more herb salt

Slice the potatoes into rounds. Steam for 5-10 minutes until tender. Drain and toss with onion and parsley. Toss with Red Wine Dressing. Place salad at centre of a large serving platter. Chill while preparing remaining ingredients.

Salad:
12 sprigs watercress
2 large tomatoes in wedges
1 medium cucumber, peeled and sliced
6 radishes
1 green pepper in rings
6 slices cooked beetroot
150g feta (cow, goat, sheep),
  coarsely crumbled

12 large black olives
6 anchovy fillets, washed
  and coarsely chopped
1 tsp oreganum

White Wine Dressing:
½ cup white wine vinegar
¼ cup olive oil combined with
  ¼ cup vegetable oil

Cover the potato salad with the feta and olives. Surround it with the vegetables and anchovies in artistic array. Sprinkle the salad with the oreganum.

Just before serving prepare the White Wine Dressing, place the vinegar in a blender or bowl and gradually beat in the oil until thick. Pour it over the non-potato salad. Serve immediately.

- *Hot and Cold Fish* •
- *Pita Bread, Taco Shells or Pasta* •
- *Carrot Stix* •

Ideal for warm weather, there are several ways — and temperatures — at which this dish can be prepared and served. The fish can be marinated raw in the dressing, then tossed with the remaining ingredients, or the fish can be cooked with the vegetables and then tossed with the dressing. If you don't like the prospect of garlic, add toasted sesame seeds or another flavourful element to the dressing.

Preparation Plan
- steam fish and vegetables; prepare dressing and toss
- cook pasta or set out option
- slice carrots, and serve

Hot and Cold Fish

600-800g fish steaks or fillets
½ cup chopped onions
3 chopped tomatoes
1 small red pepper, sliced
1 small green pepper, sliced
½ small cauliflower, in segments
2 crumbled bay leaves
6 black peppercorns

Dressing:
⅓ cup lemon juice
¼ cup olive oil
2 tbs tomato paste
2 tbs chopped parsley
1-2 tsp finely chopped fresh
   chillies (optional)
1 tsp finely chopped garlic

Place water in a saucepan ready for use with steamer. Add the bay leaves and peppercorns. Cover with steamer and then fish and vegetables. Steam for 5-8 minutes until tender.

Meanwhile prepare the Dressing: Beat the lemon juice and olive oil with a fork or whisk until blended. Once the fish and vegetables are cooked drizzle ⅔ cup of the strained steaming liquid into the Dressing, stirring constantly. Beat in the tomato paste, garlic, parsley, chillies and herb salt. Pour over the fish mixture and allow to sit at room temperature until serving time. This then may be lightly reheated if preferred.

Pita Bread, Taco Shells or Pasta
pita bread or taco shells or pasta

Either cook or drain pasta, or set out bread or shells, and serve.

Carrot Stix
carrots

Slice into sticks and serve.

- *Pickled Fish* •
- *Hot Potato* •
- *Silver Salad* •

This recipe is somewhat of a cheat since its time requirements are minimal but it does need to be prepared 24 hours, or even up to a week, in advance. The fish also makes a wonderful first course for a gala dinner or as part of a buffet luncheon.

Preparation Plan
- prepare fish; chill 24 hours or longer, and serve
- cook and toss potatoes
- prepare salad, and serve

Pickled Fish

1 cup white wine vinegar or apple cider vinegar	1 tsp mustard seeds
1 cup water	1 tsp whole cloves
2 tbs olive oil	1 tsp peppercorns
1 small onion, sliced	1 kg fresh fish in 3cm pieces
2 bay leaves, crumbled	1½ tsp seasalt

Combine all the ingredients except fish and salt. Bring to the boil, then simmer, partly covered, for 30 minutes.

Meanwhile place the fish pieces in one layer on wax paper. Sprinkle with salt and let sit at room temperature for 25 minutes. Then rinse the fish to remove excess salt.

Pack the fish into a glass or earthenware casserole dish and slowly pour the hot vinegar mixture over the fish. Cool to room temperature, then cover tightly with a plastic wrap and chill for 24 hours or up to a week. Drain and serve.

Hot Potato

potatoes	parsley
Homemade Mayonnaise or sour cream or yoghurt	dill weed or seed
	herb salt

Slice or cube potatoes and steam until tender. Toss with the remaining ingredients and serve hot.

Silver Salad

chopped silverbeet	olive oil
sliced tomatoes	oreganum

Toss the vegetables and drizzle generously with olive oil; sprinkle with oreganum.

25 *Danish Macaroni Salad* *SERVES 4-6*

- *Danish Macaroni Salad with Herring or Tongue or Eggs or Tofu* •
  • *Steamed Beets* •
  • *Dill Dressing* •

A generous salad that makes for a tasty summer meal, or serve hot as winter fare. The herring (available in jars in major foodstores) and the tongue are the traditional options. In place of macaroni cooked, cubed potato could be used.

Preparation Plan
- cook macaroni and prepare salad
- prepare dressing
- steam beets, and serve

Danish Macaroni Salad

2 cups macaroni or rice-noodles
lettuce
1 small telegraph cucumber,
  peeled and cubed
1 cup sliced mushrooms
½ cup chopped gherkins

3 spring onions, chopped
protein options:
  3-4 pickled herrings, chopped
  400g cooked tongue, sliced
  4 hard-boiled eggs, chopped
  2 blocks tofu, cubed

Cook macaroni according to packet directions. To cook rice-noodles see Cook's Tips. Drain.

Toss with the remaining ingredients. Toss with dressing and serve.

Dill Dressing

1 cup sour cream or Savoury Tofu Whip
½ cup Homemade Mayonnaise

3 tbs chopped fresh dill
2 tsp curry powder

Beat all the ingredients together until smooth and creamy.

Steamed Beets

3-4 large beetroot

Slice into quarters and steam for 10-15 minutes until tender.

• *Summer Tacos or Winter Tacos*
with myriad accompaniments and protein options •

Tacos are crisp cornmeal "envelopes", gluten-free and widely available. Wholemeal pita breads could be used instead. The idea is for individual dishes of raw or cooked vegetables, a sauce or topping and other accompaniments to be presented, with each diner filling his own tacos to suit. Allow about 3 per person depending on the heartiness of the fillings.

Preparation Plan
- prepare choice of sauce, topping, vegetables, protein options
- put out taco shells, and serve

Summer Tacos

taco shells	options:
alfalfa sprouts	raw or toasted nuts/seeds
shredded lettuce	grilled tempeh or tofu, cubed
Salsa Salad	sour cream or grated cheese
½ avocado per person	fresh cooked or tinned fish
Mayonnaise or mustard or relish	bacon, ham or salami
	chicken livers or left-over cooked meat

Serve as outlined above. For heartier appetites provide one or more of the options.

Winter Tacos

Mexicali Sauce (below)	herb salt to taste
cauliflower	alfalfa and mung sprouts
cabbage	options:
few tsp cold-pressed oil	as for Summer Tacos
few tsp cumin or coriander	

Prepare Mexicali Sauce. While simmering, steam cabbage and cauliflower until lightly cooked. Toss with oil, cumin (or coriander) and herb salt to taste. Accompany with sprouts and serve as outlined above.

Many of the options listed — tofu, meat, etc. — may be cooked in with the Sauce if preferred.

Mexicali Sauce

2 cups chopped tomato	2 tsp oreganum
1 cup Vegetable Stock	1 tsp each of:
(or use all tomatoes)	paprika
1 tbs molasses	basil
lots of garlic!	cinnamon
1 onion, chopped	cumin
1 stick celery, chopped	coriander
½ green pepper, chopped	dash of cayenne
2 carrots, diced	rice flour or other
3 bay leaves	

Bring all the ingredients to the boil and simmer for 20 minutes or longer. Whisk in flour to thicken. (Makes about 3 cups.)

- *Walnut Mushroom Pâté* •
- *Crudités* •
- *Bread and Cheese or Tofu Platter* •

Ah! the evocative sensuality this type of meal carries. Simple foods to be selected, plucked and nibbled on at one's own timing and discretion.

Preparation Plan
- prepare pâté
- prepare crudités
- arrange platter, and serve

Walnut Mushroom Pâté

olive oil or butter
1 large onion, chopped
2 cups chopped mushrooms
1-2 cloves garlic, diced

1½ cups walnuts
1 tsp marjoram or basil
¼ tsp sage
herb salt

In oil fry onion, mushrooms and garlic until tender, but not brown.

Grind walnuts in a blender, then whizz in the vegetables until well combined. Add Vegetable Stock or oil to thin if necessary. Taste for seasoning. Serve as is or chill.

Crudités

carrots
cucumber

gherkins
cauliflower

Slice the vegetables and arrange attractively.

Bread and Cheese or Tofu Platter

Vitalia cornbread
sourdough rye
sesame seed rice crackers

goat camembert
sheep's milk feta or Savoury Tofu Whip
   as a dip for the crudites

Arrange attractively and serve.

• Hummus — chickpea topping •
• Hot Pot Veg. •
• Grated Carrot Salad •

To make hummus, a pâté-like Arab chickpea side-dish, is a simple process but one which takes advance planning. Chickpeas need to be soaked overnight, cooked in the morning (using the method below you need only half an hour at home to accomplish this), then puree and season at dinnertime. Hummus may be served hot, cold or at room temperature. It stores well for several days, covered and refrigerated.

Preparation Plan

- soak chickpeas overnight; cook them in the morning; at dinnertime puree and season
- steam vegetables
- prepare salad, and serve

Hummus

1 cup raw chickpeas	about ½ cup chickpea cooking water
	½ small green pepper, chopped
1 small onion, chopped	3 tbs chopped parsley
3-6 cloves garlic, peeled	1-2 cloves garlic, chopped (optional)
½ cup tahini	2-3 tbs natural soy sauce
3 tbs lemon juice	1 tsp paprika

Soak chickpeas overnight in ample water.

In the morning drain them. Completely cover with fresh water, and add the onion and garlic. Bring to the boil, partly covered, and simmer for 30 minutes. Return to the boil, cover, turn off the heat, and cover top and sides of pan with a thick towel to trap in the heat. Leave undisturbed for one hour or longer. Drain and reserve liquid.

Whizz in a blender the chickpeas and remaining ingredients, blending in about ½ cup hot chickpea water until thick and smooth. Place in a serving bowl and sprinkle with chopped parsley.

Hot Pot Veg.

potatoes, coarsely chopped	courgettes, in chunks
silverbeet, shredded	

Steam potatoes until almost cooked. Top with silverbeet and courgettes, and continue to steam until all are tender.

Grated Carrot Salad

3 large carrots, grated	1 tsp honey
2 tbs apple cider vinegar	1 tsp grated peeled ginger root

Combine all the ingredients. Cover and let marinate at room temperature, stirring occasionally, for 10-15 minutes.

29 *Seafood Spaghetti* *SERVES 4-5*

- *Spaghetti* •
- *Seafood Sauce* •
- *Steamed Greens* •

Seafood can be absurdly expensive but a modest amount of less costly varieties can richly flavour this delicious dish.

Preparation Plan
- cook spaghetti
- prepare sauce
- steam greens, and serve

Spaghetti

about 300g spaghetti, spinach or rice-noodles   2 tbs olive oil

Cook according to packet instructions (for rice-noodles see Cook's Tips). Drain. Toss with olive oil and serve.

Seafood Sauce

1¾ cups cream or coconut cream	2 tsp oreganum
¾ cup sliced mushrooms	½ tsp nutmeg
¾ cup cubed carrots	1 cup fish chunks
¼ cup chopped parsley	1 cup chopped squid pieces
3 chopped spring onions	1 cup mussels
2 tsp basil	

While noodles are cooking, prepare the sauce. Bring all the ingredients to the boil, then turn immediately to low and simmer for 10 minutes or more until tender. Taste for seasoning, and sprinkle in the rice flour if more thickening is necessary.

Steamed Greens

spinach	green beans or courgettes
broccoli	

Roughly chop the spinach and leave the broccoli and beans in large pieces. Steam for about 5 minutes until crisply tender.

30 Spaghetti and "Meat" balls SERVES 4-6

- Italian Tomato Sauce •
- Tofu "Meat"balls •
- Spaghetti •
- Tossed Salad •

Meatballs are supposed to be an Italian-American invention, meat being very expensive in Italy. This dish is impressive served on a large oval platter with the "meat"balls covered in sauce at the centre and surrounded by noodles.

Preparation Plan
- prepare sauce
- prepare "meat"balls
- cook spaghetti
- toss salad, and serve

Italian Tomato Sauce

4 cups chopped tomatoes	½ small onion
3 tbs miso or marmite	2-4 cloves garlic
3 tbs olive oil	2 tsp basil
1 tbs apple cider vinegar	2 tsp oreganum
2 tsp brown sugar	¼ tsp nutmeg

Whizz all the ingredients in a blender. Pour them into a saucepan and bring to the boil. Simmer for 15 minutes or longer until rich, dark and flavourful. Taste for seasoning.

Tofu "Meat"balls

2 blocks tofu	1 tsp diced garlic
2 eggs, beaten	2 tsp oreganum
½ cup fine breadcrumbs	2 tsp basil
3 tbs natural soy sauce	1 tsp mixed herbs
¼ cup finely chopped onion	¼ tsp nutmeg
¼ cup chopped parsley	
3 tbs Parmesan cheese (optional)	olive oil

While the sauce simmers, prepare the balls. Mash the tofu and stir in the remaining ingredients. Form into 3cm balls and fry in the oil until well browned. Cover with sauce and cook gently over a low heat for 10 minutes or more.

Spaghetti

spaghetti or rice flour vermicelli noodles

Cook to packet instructions. See Cook's Tips for rice-noodle cooking method.

Tossed Salad

lettuce	basil
cucumber	herb salt
sliced mushrooms	freshly ground pepper
olive oil	

Toss all the ingredients.

31 Pasta Perfecto

SERVES 4

• Pasta — wheat, spinach, rice or buckwheat noodles •
• Casentino Walnut Sauce •
• Broccoli Salad •

A super-quick light meal of distinctive Italian ambience. Simply cook pasta and serve alongside, or covered with a bellisimo walnut sauce. Casentino is the name of the river along which Italy's finest walnuts are grown. The broccoli salad may be served raw or the broccoli steamed, then tossed with the dressing.

Preparation Plan

- prepare sauce
- cook pasta
- prepare broccoli, and serve

Casentino Walnut Sauce

2 cups Vegetable or chicken Stock
or part cream or coconut cream
½ cup ground walnuts
¼ cup whole or coarsley chopped walnuts
or whole pinenuts
1 large red pepper, sliced
12 whole baby mushrooms
2 carrots, diced
1 cup peas or
chopped green beans
4 spring onions, chopped
handful chopped parsley
3 cloves garlic, chopped
3 tbs natural soy sauce
2 tbs rice flour or other
2 tbs olive oil
1 tbs apple cider vinegar
1 tsp honey
1 tsp dill seed
1 tsp basil

Bring all the ingredients to the boil and simmer gently for 10 minutes or more, until tender and flavourful. Taste for seasoning.

Pasta

choice of ribbon or spaghetti noodles: wholemeal, rice, spinach or buckwheat

Cook to packet instructions or use the following method for more delicate rice or buckwheat-flour noodles. Bring water to the boil and add the noodles. As soon as water returns to the boil remove from heat, cover, and let sit for 5-8 minutes (depending on size of noodles). Drain and serve.

Broccoli Salad

small raw or steamed broccoli pieces
2 tbs olive oil
1 tbs lemon juice
1 tsp oreganum
dash herb salt

Toss all the ingredients. If using broccoli raw, prepare the salad before the pasta and chill, covered, to marinate. If serving as a hot vegetable, prepare after the pasta and serve promptly.

Bami Goreng

- *Bami Goreng with Egg or Tofu/Tempeh or Fish or Meat* •
  • *Peanut Sauce* •
- *Cucumber Sambal and side-dishes*

Exotic to present yet easy on the pocketbook and tastebuds. Bami Goreng is the name for a flavourful Indonesian noodle dish. Nasi Goreng follows the same method of preparation but uses cooked rice instead of noodles. Traditionally strips of omelette, lean pork or steak are tossed in with the noodles, but tofu, tempeh or fish could be used instead of, or in addition to, the egg. Here the dish is accompanied by a peanut sauce and a colourful array of salad vegetables and condiments best displayed in a series of small bowls. Adults and children alike seem to enjoy this select-a-topping style.

Preparation Plan
- boil noodles; cook with vegetables
- prepare sauce
- prepare sambal and side-dishes

Bami Goreng

ribbon or spaghetti-type noodles:
  wholemeal, rice or buckwheat
cold-pressed oil
4-6 eggs (depending on use of
  protein options)
1 tsp coriander
herb salt
handful parsley
1 medium onion, sliced
4 spring onions, sliced
1 red pepper, sliced

small cauliflower segments
chopped cabbage
3 cloves garlic
optional extras:
  cubed tofu or tempeh
  thin slices pork or beef steak
  cubed fish
1 tsp paprika
1 tsp coriander
1 tsp Chinese 5-spice
2 tbs natural soy sauce

Cook noodles and drain. If using rice or buckwheat-flour noodles, bring ample water to the boil; add noodles and return to boil. Then remove from heat and cover; allow to sit for 5-8 minutes until lightly cooked.

Heat oil in a sturdy frypan or wok. Beat eggs with coriander, herb salt and parsley. Pour into the pan and cook as for an omelette until lightly set. Remove from pan, cool, and slice into thin strips.

Heat more oil in the pan and stir-fry vegetables and garlic over a medium-high heat until crisply tender, adding any of the optional extras to also cook.

Stir in remaining spices and drained noodles and cook for 5-10 minutes, or longer. Toss in the omelette strips, turn out onto a serving plate and sprinkle with soy sauce.

While cooking noodles and vegetables, prepare the sauce, then the condiments.

Peanut Sauce

2½ cups Vegetable Stock
4-5 tbs pea flour or other
¼ cup peanut butter
2 tbs natural soy sauce
3cm peeled ginger root

1-3 cloves garlic
1 tsp coriander
1 tsp garam masala
pinch cayenne

Whizz all the ingredients in a blender. Pour into a saucepan and bring to the boil. Simmer for 10 minutes or longer.

Remember this recipe for serving over vegetables, when layering casseroles, or use cold as a dip or dressing. Great for barbecues too.

Cucumber Sambal (salad-relish) and side-dishes

1 medium cucumber
2 tbs apple cider vinegar
2 tbs honey
1 tsp paprika
fresh chilli peppers, finely chopped
  or tobasco or chilli powder to taste

herb salt

other side-dishes:
  grated carrot
  roasted peanuts
  banana chips (purchased)

Once prepared, allow as much time as possible for the cucumber to marinate in the dressing.

Peel and thinly slice the cucumber. Toss with the remaining ingredients, cover and chill.

Remember to handle fresh chillies with care. Wear gloves while chopping or otherwise be careful not to rub your eyes until your hands are thoroughly cleaned.

- *Yellow Rice* -
- *Cuban Stewed Vegetables with Egg or Tofu/Tempeh or Fish or Meat* -
- *Peanut and Cauliflower Salad* -

This premise of a flavourful sauce, cooked with ample vegetables and served with a protein, is one you can make easy and imaginative use of in a multiplicity of ways. Take any of the sauce recipes from this book, likewise complement and recombine, and design your own original creations. Here the rice is very attractive served on a large platter and draped with a thick stripe or two of stew.

Preparation Plan
- cook rice
- prepare ' stew
- prepare salad, and serve

Yellow Rice

1½ cups brown rice
2¾ cups water
2 tsp mild curry powder

½ tsp turmeric
herb salt

Bring all the ingredients to the boil, covered. Boil for 10 minutes undisturbed, then turn heat off and cover and surround saucepan with a thick towel to trap in heat. Let sit undisturbed for 25 minutes or longer.

Cuban Stewed Vegetables

olive oil
5 large tomatoes, chopped
1 large green pepper, sliced
1 large onion, sliced
1 cup peas
1 cup corn
1 tsp diced garlic
1 tsp diced ginger root
1-3 chillies, chopped
3 tbs peanut butter

2 tsp cumin powder
herb salt

protein options:
   4 hard-boiled eggs, halved
   cubed tofu or tempeh
   fish chunks
   sliced quick-cooking pork
    or beef steak
   chicken breast, sliced

Peanut and Cauliflower Salad

peanuts, coarsely chopped
cauliflower
cucumber, peeled and cubed

olive oil
herb salt

Toast peanuts. Chop cauliflower into small pieces. Toss with cucumber, oil and nuts.

- *Jambalaya* •
- *Carrots in Sherry* •
- *Sliced Tomatoes* •

Jambalaya is a Creole specialty, a one-pot porridgey rice-dish well flavoured with seafood and sometimes smoked ham. It is ample enough to be served with a simple display of raw vegetables or add a quick side-dish like the Carrots in Sherry.

Preparation Plan
- prepare rice dish
- cook carrots
- prepare tomatoes, and serve

Jambalaya

¼ cup cold-pressed oil	3 cups mixed fish chunks,
1 large onion, chopped	mussels, and squid rings
4 spring onions (including 8cm of	¼ cup chopped parsley
green tops), chopped	1 tsp paprika
1 large green pepper, chopped	1 tsp bouquet garni
3 sticks celery, chopped	1 tsp or more herb salt
1 tsp finely chopped garlic	dash-¼ tsp cayenne
2 cups brown rice	3¾ cups water

In a large heavy saucepan heat the oil over a medium heat and cook the vegetables and garlic for about 5 minutes, until soft but not brown.

Meanwhile place dry rice in a blender and whizz briefly to crack. Slice the seafood.

Stir the rice into cooking vegetables until well combined. Add remaining ingredients and bring to the boil, covered. Cook undisturbed over a brisk heat for 10 minutes. Turn heat off, and with a thick towel, cover the top and sides of pan to trap in heat. Leave undisturbed for 20 minutes or longer.

Carrots In Sherry

6 large carrots	1 tbs honey
2 tbs sherry	1 tsp dill seed
1 tbs cold-pressed oil	herb salt

Slice the carrots lengthwise into quarters. Steam until just tender. Drain and toss with remaining ingredients.

Sliced Tomatoes

4 medium tomatoes

Slice tomatoes into rounds and arrange attractively on a serving plate.

35 *Croutons & Almond Rice*

• *Almond Rice* •
• *Crispy Tofu Croutons* •
• *Braised Vegetables* •

This is the sort of meal that gives vegetarian cooking a good reputation. Lots of crunch, texture, flavour, variety and colour. Remember the crouton idea for salads, soups and other uses.

Preparation Plan
- cook rice and prepare topping
- prepare vegetables
- prepare croutons, and serve

Almond Rice

2 cups brown rice	1 tsp herb salt
3¾ cups water	½ tsp turmeric
2 tsp curry powder	
1 tsp diced ginger root	⅔ cup sliced almonds
1 tsp Chinese 5-spice powder	dash herb salt

Bring rice, water and seasonings to the boil. Boil, covered for 10 minutes. Without at any point lifting the lid, turn off heat and with a thick towel cover and surround the pot to trap in heat. Let sit for 25 minutes or longer.

Toast nuts in a sturdy frypan. Serve rice on a large platter and cover with nuts. Sprinkle with salt and serve.

Braised Vegetables

mixed seasonal vegetables such as:	3 tbs peanut butter
brussels sprouts, cauliflower segments,	2 tbs miso or marmite
whole baby mushrooms	1 tsp tarragon
3 cups Vegetable Stock	1 tsp basil
6 tbs rice flour or other	½ tsp bouquet garni

Place all the ingredients in one large saucepan. About 15 minutes before serving time bring to the boil, then simmer for 10 minutes. Meanwhile prepare tofu.

Crispy Tofu Croutons

2 blocks tofu,	1 tsp curry powder
sliced into 2-3cm cubes	1 tsp oreganum
3 tbs rice flour	1 tsp herb salt
3 tbs sesame seeds	cold-pressed oil

Combine all the ingredients except tofu in a plastic or paper bag. Add several tofu cubes at a time and shake to coat evenly. Fry in oil over a medium heat (or baste and bake in the oven) for 5-10 minutes to crispen. Cook in batches and keep warm.

- Pineapple Rice •
- Vegetables in Creamy Dill Sauce •
- Celery Stix •

Another simple, nourishing and scrumptious rice-based menu. For heartier appetites cubes of tempeh, cheese, fish or meat may be simmered in with the rice as it cooks.

Preparation Plan
- cook rice
- prepare vegetables and sauce
- slice celery, and serve

Pineapple Rice

2 cups brown rice
3¼ cups water
250g crushed pineapple
1 tsp herb salt

½ tsp turmeric

¼ cup sesame seeds

Bring all the ingredients to the boil (except sesame seeds). Boil covered for 10 minutes and without uncovering, turn heat off. Surround and cover pot with a thick towel to trap in heat. Leave undisturbed for 30 minutes or more.

Meanwhile toast the sesame seeds. At serving time sprinkle them over the rice.

Vegetables In Creamy Dill Sauce

carrots, in sticks
courgettes, sliced
onion, sliced
mushrooms, sliced
2 cups coconut cream
5 tbs rice flour or other

3 tbs chopped parsley
1 tbs food yeast or peanut butter
1 tsp herb salt
½ tsp nutmeg

3 tbs fresh chopped dill

Bring all the ingredients — except dill — to the boil and simmer for 10-15 minutes until vegetables are tender and the sauce thick and flavourful. Stir in dill and taste for seasoning.

Celery Stix

celery

Slice celery into sticks and serve.

• *Oriental Rice Salad — hot or cold, with Tofu or Fish or Chicken* •
• *Sweet and Sour Dressing* •
• *Sprouts* •

This rice dish cum salad can be served hot or cold. If cold it may be served as a mould. Simply pack the mixture into a decorative mould or a bowl, cover and chill for at least 2 hours. Unmould and surround with lettuce or watercress. If you are using fresh fish or chicken in the rice mixture, chunks or slices may be added to cook with the rice.

Preparation Plan
- cook rice and prepare salad
- prepare dressing
- arrange sprouts, and serve

Oriental Rice Salad

2 cups brown rice
3¾ cups water
½-1 tsp herb salt

one of the following protein options:
   cubed, grilled or fried tofu
   tinned tuna or sardines
   fresh fish or chicken chunks

4 tbs olive oil
2 tbs apple cider vinegar
2 tbs prepared mustard
2 large tomatoes, sliced
¼ cup chopped spring onion
1 red pepper, sliced
2 sticks celery, sliced
2-3 courgettes, sliced

Bring water, rice and salt to the boil (raw fish or chicken may be added now). Boil covered for 10 minutes; then without uncovering turn off heat and cover the top and sides of the pan with a thick towel to trap in the heat. Let sit for 20 minutes or longer.

Combine oil, vinegar and mustard. Toss with the remaining ingredients and rice. Mound on a platter and serve.

Sweet and Sour Dressing

½ cup pineapple juice
¼ cup mayonnaise
2 tbs natural soy sauce

2 tbs apple cider vinegar
1 tsp Chinese 5-spice powder

Combine all the ingredients and serve as an accompaniment to the rice.

Sprouts

alfalfa sprouts
fenugreek sprouts

moong bean sprouts

Arrange a selection of sprouts and serve.

- *Spiced Rice* •
• *Salad Sideboard: Walnut and Courgette,*
Tomato and Chilli, Pawpaw or Avocado and Ginger •

A simple rice dish — which can be attractively set in a mould — accompanied by a colourful rainbow of salad dishes. Perfect for warm weather or adjust the concept to include side-dishes of steamed vegetables, and vegetables cooked in sauce, for colder evenings.

Preparation Plan
- cook rice
- prepare salads; marinate, and serve

Spiced Rice

2 cups brown rice	1 tsp cardamom
3¾ cups water	½ tsp turmeric
2 tsp paprika	½-1 tsp herb salt
1 tsp curry powder	

Bring all the ingredients to the boil, and boil covered for 10 minutes. Without lifting the lid turn heat off and cover top and sides of pot with a thick towel to trap in heat. Leave undisturbed for 20 minutes or more. Meanwhile prepare salads.

If you wish to serve the rice as a mould: lightly oil a bowl, mould or oval casserole dish and lightly pack in rice to which 2 tablespoons butter or oil has been added. Cover with a tea towel and let sit in a warm place for 10 minutes.

Salad Sideboard

Walnut and Courgette:

3 courgettes, sliced	3 tbs cold-pressed oil
½ cup coarsely chopped walnuts	1 tsp cumin powder
½ cup sliced mushrooms	herb salt

Combine all the ingredients and cover. Allow the most time possible — 30 minutes is ideal — for the salads to marinate at room temperature for best flavour.

Tomato and Chilli:

2 large tomatoes, chopped	¼-½ tsp finely chopped garlic
½ cup fresh green peas	¼ cup pineapple juice or use
2 spring onions, chopped	½ lemon juice ½ cold-pressed oil
1 fresh chilli, diced	

Prepare as above.

Pawpaw or Avocado and Ginger:

1-2 avocados, peeled and cubed	1 tsp powdered ginger or
or 1 pawpaw, peeled and cubed	1 tbs grated peeled ginger root
1 tbs lemon juice	½ tsp Chinese 5-spice

Prepare as above.

Millet in a Skillet

- *Savoury Mushroom Millet — with Bacon or Sardines* •
- *Tomato Topping* •
- *Sesame Broccoli Salad* •

Millet makes it to the dinner table. Try and remember to soak it overnight — although not imperative, this makes for a creamier texture. Of course unsweetened left-over cooked breakfast cereal can be used in the same fashion.

Preparation Plan
- soak millet for 8 hours or more; cook
- prepare tomato topping and serve over millet
- prepare salad, and serve

Savoury Mushroom Millet

1¼ cups ground millet or millet flakes	½ cup sliced mushrooms
2½ cups water	4 slices bacon, chopped or 2 tins sardines
¼ cup rice flour or other	1 tsp coriander
2 tbs cold-pressed oil	¼ tsp turmeric

Soak millet and rice flour in water for 8 hours or more.

In a large cast-iron frypan fry the mushrooms and optional bacon in oil until cooked. Stir in coriander and fry for one minute.

Stir in optional sardines, millet and water and bring to the boil, adding more water if too dry. Cover and turn off heat, then cover with a thick towel to trap in heat and leave undisturbed for at least 10 minutes or until ready to top with Tomato Topping.

Tomato Topping

3 tbs olive oil	2 tbs natural soy sauce
3 large tomatoes, chopped	1 tbs molasses
2 sticks celery, sliced	1 tbs apple cider vinegar
1 large carrot, diced	2 tsp oreganum
1 large onion, sliced	½ tsp cinnamon
1 green pepper, sliced	

Bring all the ingredients to the boil and simmer for 20 minutes or until tender. Pour over the cooked millet and serve.

Sesame Broccoli Salad

raw (or steamed) broccoli segments	1 tsp honey
2 tbs sesame seeds	herb salt
1 tbs lemon juice	

Toast sesame seeds until golden brown. While hot toss with honey, lemon juice and salt. Toss with broccoli until well combined.

- *Buckwheat Risotto* •
- *Eggplant Fritters* •
- *Stix* •

Buckwheat is not technically a grain — despite its contradictory appearance — but is in the same family as rhubarb! People in the Middle East eat it with abandon; here it is more soberly accompanied by crisply-coated succulent eggplant and a simple selection of raw vegetables.

Preparation Plan
- prepare eggplant fritters
- prepare risotto
- prepare stix, and serve

Eggplant Fritters

2 medium-large eggplants
3 tbs cornmeal
3 tbs rice flour or other
1 tsp oreganum
½ tsp turmeric
herb salt
olive oil

Preheat oven to 200ºC. Slice eggplant at short end into 5mm slices. Combine the remaining dry ingredients in a plastic bag. Add one or two slices at a time and shake well to cover. Place in one layer in one or two large well-oiled baking pans. Drizzle with oil. Bake for 20 minutes or more until crisp.

Buckwheat Risotto

¼ cup sesame seeds
2 cups buckwheat
3½ cups Vegetable Stock
1 large onion, sliced
10 mushrooms, sliced
1-3 courgettes, sliced
1 red pepper, sliced
8 olives, chopped
2-4 cloves garlic, chopped
2 tsp oreganum
herb salt
2 tbs food yeast

Toast the sesame seeds and buckwheat without oil in a heavy skillet until well browned (this gives it a nutty flavour). Add remaining ingredients, except food yeast, and bring to the boil for 5 minutes, covered. Keep covered with lid, turn off heat and with a thick towel cover top and sides of saucepan to trap in heat. Leave undisturbed for 10 minutes or more. Place on serving platter and sprinkle with yeast.

Stix

carrots
celery
beetroot

Slice into tidy matchstick pieces and serve fancifully, teepee style, on a platter with a radish rose or herb sprig at the centre.

41   *Some Like It Sour*

- *Buckwheat with Egg or Nuts or Fish or Meat* •
- *Green Beans in Sour Mustard Sauce* •
- *Reds* •

This meal has as many variations as you have thoughts. Rice, barley or noodles can be used in place of buckwheat. Combinations like carrot and cauliflower, eggplant and broccoli, pumpkin and brussels sprouts, can be used in place of the beans and parsnips. Experiment with different sauce recipes in this book as an accompaniment.

Preparation Plan
- cook buckwheat and protein option
- steam vegetables and toss with sauce
- slice vegetables, and serve

Buckwheat with Protein Option

one of the following protein options:
- 4 eggs, hard-boiled or cooked as an omelette, then sliced into strips
- ½-¾ cup toasted nuts or seeds
- 1-2 chicken breasts, sliced
- 300-400g veal or beef fillet, sliced
- 300-400g fresh fish, sliced

2 cups buckwheat
3¾ cups water
1-2 tsp curry powder
1 tsp bouquet garni
½ tsp allspice
herb salt
1 medium onion, chopped
3 cloves garlic, chopped

Choose one of the protein options. If using eggs or nuts toss these in with the buckwheat once it is cooked. If using raw meat or fish this may be brought to the boil with the buckwheat and other ingredients for 5 minutes. Turn heat off and cover top and sides of the pan with a thick towel to trap in heat. Let sit undisturbed for 10 minutes.

Green Beans and Parsnips with Sour Mustard Sauce

green beans
parsnips
1 egg

¼ cup apple cider vinegar
2 tbs brown sugar
2 tbs prepared hot or mild mustard

Slice parsnips into rounds and keep beans whole or sliced lengthwise. Steam for about 10 minutes until tender.

Meanwhile prepare the Sauce. In the top of a double boiler combine remaining ingredients and beat until smooth. Cook over simmering, not boiling, water and heat for about 3 minutes until the sauce thickens lightly and clings to the whisk. Taste for seasoning. Place the vegetables on a heated platter and cover with sauce.

Reds

1 red capsicum
radishes

On a small plate arrange a fan of long thin capsicum slices on one side and round radish slices on the other.

---

42 *Herbcakes* *SERVES 3-4*

- *Herbcakes* -
- *Mashed Pumpkin* -
- *Curried Cauliflower* -

Herb pancakes are popular in Slavic nations — and with anyone with a fertile herb garden. Only fresh herbs can be used in this recipe. Experiment with different varieties.

Preparation Plan
- prepare pumpkin
- prepare cauliflower
- cook herbcakes, and serve

Mashed Pumpkin

pumpkin (no need to peel)

Chop pumpkin into small-medium pieces. Steam until tender and reserve the stock. Mash with a potato masher and beat in reserved stock until desired consistency. Keep warm until serving time.

Curried Cauliflower

cauliflower	1-2 tbs mild curry powder
celery, angle-cut	1 tbs toasted sesame seeds
½ cup yoghurt (cow, goat) or	
coconut cream	spinach leaves

Reserve spinach as a raw garnish. Steam vegetables until just tender. Toss with the remaining ingredients and keep warm until serving time (the flavour improves with sitting). Serve surrounded with torn chunks of raw spinach.

Herbcakes

3 eggs	½ cup finely chopped dill or mint
1 cup finely chopped parsley	herb salt
½ cup finely chopped spring onions	cold-pressed oil

While vegetables are cooking prepare herbcakes.

Beat eggs well, then stir in the remaining ingredients. Heat oil over medium heat and fry mixture in 2 tablespoon amounts making about 16 small cakes. Cook for 2-3 minutes on each side. Keep warm until serving time.

43 *Indonesian Fritters* SERVES 4

- *Corn and Spinach Fritters* •
- *Kumara (Sweet Potato)* •
- *Sprout Platter with Tangy Topping* •

Fritters can be a successful way of slipping vegetables into children. These have the additional value, however, of adult-appeal and cook's time-conservation. The fritters are exotically Indonesian without being too hot or heady. Make extra for yummy snacks and lunches.

Preparation Plan
- prepare fritters
- steam kumara
- prepare sprouts and topping, and serve

Corn and Spinach Fritters

1 bunch spinach	½-⅔ cup rice flour or other
2 cups corn	2 tsp coriander
3 spring onions, chopped	1 tsp chopped garlic
1 cup coconut cream	herb salt
2 eggs	

Wash, drain and chop the spinach. Combine with the remaining ingredients to get a thickish pancake batter consistency. Fry over a medium-high heat, for a few minutes on each side. Keep fritters warm as you cook subsequent batches.

Steam kumara while frying fritters.

Kumara (Sweet Potato)

kumara

Steam kumara, whole or cut in half lengthwise, for about 10 minutes until soft.

Sprout Platter with Tangy Topping

1 or more types of bean sprouts	Homemade Mayonnaise, Vinaigrette or
chilli sauce or other tangy relish	other dressing

Combine sauce or relish with choice of dressing: about 1-2 parts sauce to 2 parts dressing. Serve in a small bowl at the centre of a platter of arranged bean sprouts.

44 *Eat Up Your Breakfast* SERVES 4

- *Polenta Rounds* •
- *Vegetables Almondine* •
- *Tomato Wedges* •

A cagey way of both using up left-over porridge and serving a classic Italian dish. Here the porridge is made from cornmeal ("polenta" in Italian) though unsweetened cooked oats or ground rice would also work. The porridge is spread thin, chilled, cut into rounds and cooked plain or with garlic, onion and parmesan. Make extra cereal in the morning to serve for breakfast. Your family will never guess when later that day they are served their breakfast for dinner.

Preparation Plan
- cook cereal; chill; slice and fry
- steam vegetables; toast almonds and combine
- prepare tomatoes, and serve

Polenta Rounds

1½ cups fine cornmeal	2-4 cloves garlic, chopped
3 cups water	1 tsp paprika
dash salt	1 tsp basil
	1 tsp oreganum
olive oil	parmesan or crumbled feta
1 large onion, sliced	(cow, goat or sheep)

In the morning or up to 2 days before, cook cornmeal as for porridge: bring to the boil (adding more water if necessary), cover, turn off heat, and let sit undisturbed for 15 minutes or longer. Spoon evenly to a 10mm depth into an ungreased pan. Refrigerate for at least 2 hours until very firm.

At dinnertime fry onion and garlic in oil over a low heat until very tender. Fry in the paprika and herbs. Remove to a heated serving platter.

Meanwhile with an 8cm cookie cutter or glass, cut polenta into rounds. Add more oil to the pan and fry on both sides until golden brown. Remove to the serving platter and surround with onion mixture. Sprinkle rounds with cheese and keep warm until serving time.

Vegetables Almondine

whole baby carrots	½ cup almonds, coarsely chopped
brussels sprouts, halved	herb salt
green beans or lengthwise-sliced courgettes	

While polenta rounds are cooking steam the vegetables for about 10 minutes until tender. Toast the almonds. Drain the vegetables and toss with nuts and herb salt.

Tomato Wedges

3 large tomatoes	1 tsp basil
olive oil	

Slice tomatoes into wedges. Arrange on a serving plate and drizzle with oil. Sprinkle with basil, and serve.

- *Country Corn Cakes* •
- *Caponata* •
- *Radishes and Cucumber Boats* •

This cornmeal pancake variation originated in the Eastern United States. You could serve them at breakfast, but sneaking them onto the dinner menu should cause no complaint. The caponata is a classic Mediterranean dish profuse with succulent vegetables. The Italians frequently use cornmeal in bread, dumplings and other dishes so the composition of this menu is not disconsonant. Caponata is delicious hot, or cold when it is traditionally served as a relish.

Preparation Plan
- prepare caponata
- prepare corn cakes
- prepare raw vegetables, and serve

Caponata

1 large eggplant	3 tbs olive oil
1 large onion, cubed	3 tbs apple cider vinegar
2 sticks celery, cubed	2 tbs brown sugar
3 large carrots, cubed	4 anchovies, diced (optional)
8 olives, chopped	3 bay leaves
2 cups chopped tomatoes	herb salt

Chop eggplant into 10mm cubes. Place it and all other ingredients in a large pot and bring to the boil. Simmer, covered, for 25 minutes or more.

Taste for seasoning.

Country Corn Cakes

1½ cups fine cornmeal	4 large eggs, separated
1½ cups rice flour or other	3 tbs cold-pressed oil
1½ tsp baking powder or	½-1 tsp herb salt
1 tbs Prepared Yeast	butter or margarine
3 cups buttermilk or goat yoghurt	

Combine all dry ingredients. Beat in the milk, egg yolks, oil and salt. Beat egg whites until stiff peaks form. Fold them gently, but thoroughly, into the cornmeal mixture.

Heat an electric frypan to 180°C or a sturdy cast-iron frypan over medium heat until a drop of water flicked on it splutters and quickly evaporates. Lightly grease with butter or margarine. Spoon on batter to make about 18 x 10cm cakes. Cook for about 3 minutes on each side until golden and crisp.

Radishes and Cucumber Boats

radishes	cucumber

Arrange a small platter of cucumbers sliced into stick or boat lengths. The whole radishes may each be decorated by making thin cuts almost to the base, then slicing again at right angles to the initial slices.

- *Salad Fritters*
- *Hazelnut Sauce*
- *Florida Beetroot*

Tarator is a Turkish hazelnut sauce traditionally served with cold lobster or shrimp. Try it on other hot or cold, mildly-flavoured proteins like fish, chicken, tofu or chickpeas. Here it is served with crunchy hashed brown-like fritters kept simple to complement the rich sauce. Of course you could choose a different sauce or relish and add eggs, cubed tofu, chopped fish, etc to the fritters to make them more substantial.

Preparation Plan
- prepare sauce
- cook beetroot
- cook fritters, and serve

Hazelnut Sauce

1½ cups hazelnuts or walnuts, ground
¾ cup fresh breadcrumbs
1-3 tsp finely chopped garlic
½ tsp crushed, dried hot red pepper
½ tsp paprika
dash seasalt

dash cayenne
¼ cup olive oil
⅓ cup red wine vinegar
3 tbs Homemade Mayonnaise
4-6 tbs cold water

Toss the nuts, breadcrumbs, garlic, seasonings and salt until combined. Pour in the olive oil and vinegar and mash until absorbed. Stir in mayonnaise. Beat in water a tablespoon at a time using only enough to thin the sauce sufficiently to hold its shape lightly in a spoon. Taste for seasoning and chill until ready to use. If the sauce becomes too firm beat in a teaspoon or two of cold water to soften it.

Florida Beetroot

beetroot, scrubbed
onions, sliced in rings
1 cup orange juice
grated rind of 1 orange

1½ tbs arrowroot
1 tbs cold-pressed oil
1 tbs apple cider vinegar
1 tbs honey

Slice and steam beetroot until tender. Meanwhile combine remaining ingredients. Bring to the boil, stirring constantly. Turn off heat, stir in hot drained beetroot. Keep warm until serving time.

Salad Fritters

2½ cups grated potato
1 cup grated carrot
1 cup grated marrow or courgette
1 tsp paprika

1 tsp curry powder
herb salt
bacon fat, butter or margarine

Combine all the ingredients except the bacon fat or option. Heat the fat over a medium heat until very hot. Fry mixture in small thin patties; cook thoroughly on each side until crisp and potato is cooked.

If preferred the mixture could be cooked as one mass. Toss and flip with abandon and mash it into a presentable round before serving. Slice into wedges.

Eggplant Pancake

- *Stewed Sunflower Tomatoes* •
- *Eggplant Pancake* •
- *Vegetable Fingers* •

Minus the vegetables (or with them) this is a very nice everyday pancake mixture. Remember it for breakfasts. The eggplant variation can be made as small individual pancakes or as one large version as outlined here.

Preparation Plan
- stew tomatoes
- prepare pancakes
- slice vegetables, and serve

Stewed Sunflower Tomatoes

⅓ cup sunflower seed kernels
5-6 large tomatoes, chopped
3 tbs sherry or Vegetable Stock
1 tbs molasses

1 tbs miso or marmite
2 tsp oreganum
½ tsp cinnamon

Toast the sunflower seed kernels. Reserve 2 tablespoons for garnish. Add the remaining ingredients to the seeds in the pan and cook for 20-30 minutes over a low heat until thick and well-flavoured. Place in a serving bowl and sprinkle with reserved seeds.

Eggplant Pancake

3 tbs olive oil
1 large eggplant, cubed
1 green pepper, sliced
1 large onion, sliced

1 egg

1 cup milk
1 cup rice flour or other
2 tbs cold-pressed oil
2 tsp baking powder
herb salt
¼ tsp nutmeg

In a 25cm cast-iron, non-stick or electric frypan saute the vegetables in olive oil for 5-8 minutes until just tender.

Beat the egg. Stir in the remaining ingredients. With heat at medium (160ºC) pour pancake mixture over vegetables. When pancake is firm enough to be flipped, turn over and cook other side.

Vegetable Fingers

celery

courgette

Slice vegetables into sticks and serve.

- *Crunchy Croquettes* •
- *Lemon Stewed Vegetables* •
- *Strips* •

These croquettes are of Algerian origin. If you have the time they are very good made with mashed cooked chickpeas in place of half the bread called for. In any case the recipe is great for using up stale or left-over bread.

Preparation Plan
- soak bread and prepare croquettes
- stew vegetables
- slice strips, and serve

Crunchy Croquettes

3 cups breadcrumbs (cornbread or other)
¼-½ cup milk (cow, goat, soy,
   coconut cream)
3 eggs
1 cup grated gruyere or crumbled feta
   (sheep, goat) or other tasty cheese

3 tbs parsley
2 tsp coriander
½ tsp cinnamon
cold-pressed oil

Combine the breadcrumbs with the milk until well moistened but not dripping. Beat in the eggs until well blended. Stir in the remaining ingredients until smooth. Taste for seasoning.

Moistening your hands frequently with cold water, shape the mixture into slightly flattened balls about 3cm in diameter. Either fry in oil or bake in a well-greased pan in a hot oven (200ºC), turning them once until crisp (about 10-15 minutes in the oven).

Lemon Stewed Vegetables

2-3 cups mixed seasonal vegetables
   (such as cauliflower, courgette, pumpkin)
1 small lemon, sliced
2 cups Vegetable Stock
4 tbs rice flour or other

2 tbs natural soy sauce
1 tbs honey
2 tsp coriander
1 tsp tarragon
½ tsp nutmeg

Bring all the ingredients to the boil, then simmer for 10-15 minutes until thick and flavourful.

Strips

red pepper

Slice into strips and serve.

- *Dutch Flatties* •
- *Capsicum Sauce* •
- *Cucumber Platter* •

Eight large crêpés are spread and stacked with a creamy vegetable sauce. Serve on a round platter and slice into attractive pie-shaped wedges.

Preparation Plan

- prepare sauce
- prepare crêpés
- prepare cucumber, and serve

Capsicum Sauce

1 green pepper, sliced	¼ cup food yeast
1 red pepper, sliced	1 tsp bouquet garni
sliced mushrooms	½ tsp nutmeg
carrots, cubed	herb salt
3 cups Vegetable Stock or milk	3 tbs sherry
4-5 tbs rice flour	

Bring all the ingredients (except sherry) to the boil. Then turn to simmer for 15 minutes or longer while preparing the pancakes. Once simmering, stir in sherry and taste for seasoning.

Dutch Flatties

2¼ cups rice flour or other	1½ cups milk (cow, goat, soy)
4 eggs	2 tbs cold-pressed oil
herb salt	extra oil for frying

Beat all the ingredients for 2-3 minutes.

Heat a heavy 20cm frypan over a medium heat and add a little oil. Ladle in about 3 tbs batter and spread it evenly. Cook briefly and flip, cooking for about one minute. Keep warm while preparing others. Stack in between paper towels to prevent them sticking together.

When all are finished spread with vegetables and sauce, and stack, ending with a top layer of sauce. Sprinkle with paprika. Serve as above.

Cucumber Platter

lettuce	basil
cucumber	oreganum
olive oil	

On a rectangular platter arrange chunks of lettuce and cover with spears of cucumber. Drizzle with olive oil and sprinkle with basil and oreganum. Serve.

- *Spanish Omelette* •
- *Crispy Potatoes* •
- *Poppyseed Cauliflower* •

The omelette is also a great luncheon or breakfast dish, an easy (2-step, 1-pan) way to feed a number of diners. Heartier appetites can add in salami, sausage, bacon or smoked fish. The crispy potatoes are always popular and the method can be used to cook kumara or pumpkin.

Preparation Plan
- prepare potatoes
- prepare omelette
- prepare cauliflower, and serve

Crispy Potatoes

4-6 large potatoes
olive oil

turmeric

Preheat oven to 200°C.

As with all other recipes in this book, don't peel the potatoes! Slice them very thinly at their short end and place in a large oiled baking dish which doesn't squash them too much, and one that is suitable for serving at the table. Drizzle with olive oil and sprinkle with turmeric. Bake for about 30-35 minutes until tender and well browned.

Spanish Omelette

olive oil
1 large red or green pepper, sliced
3 medium courgettes, sliced
1 medium onion, sliced
2 cloves garlic, chopped
6 large eggs

2 tbs water
herb salt
1 tsp oreganum
paprika
parsley

Over a gentle heat slowly fry the vegetables in a large cast-iron or electric frypan until soft and tender.

About 15 minutes before serving beat the eggs with the water, herb salt and oreganum. Pour this mixture over the vegetables. Cook over a low heat allowing a bottom crust to form. Then lift up the crust and allow any uncooked egg to move to the bottom. When the top is almost set, sprinkle with parsley and paprika. Serve piping hot.

Poppyseed Cauliflower

large cauliflower segments
2 tsp poppyseeds

2 tsp cold-pressed oil
1 tsp prepared mustard

If serving cauliflower raw, toss with remaining ingredients and allow to sit, covered, to marinate while preparing omelette.

If serving cauliflower cooked, prepare while omelette vegetables are cooking. Steam briefly until tender, drain, toss with remaining ingredients and serve promptly.

- *Egg Foo Yung* -
- *Chinese Mushroom Sauce* -
- *5-Spice Vegetable Chow Mein* -

The popular taste and fast cooking of Chinese food — minus the MSG. The egg foo yung is of a style different to many local takeaways and is cooked as small fluffy omelettes, about 3 per person. Make sure you serve these hot and prompt. Accompany with a simple sauce, crispy noodles and vegetables. If you'd rather not fry the noodles, boil and drain them, and toss with the cooked vegetables.

Preparation Plan
- prepare sauce
- prepare vegetables and noodles
- prepare omelettes, and serve

Chinese Mushroom Sauce

2 cups chicken or Vegetable Stock	2 tbs arrowroot
1 cup sliced mushrooms	1 tsp Chinese 5-spice powder
3 tbs natural soy sauce	1 tsp coriander
3 tbs ketchup	

Place all the ingredients in a saucepan. Fifteen minutes before serving bring to the boil and simmer over lowest heat until serving. Do not reboil.

5-Spice Vegetable Chow Mein

1 large red pepper	1 tsp Chinese 5-spice
cauliflower segments	chow mein noodles or wheat or
broccoli segments	rice-flour vermicelli noodles
2 tbs cold-pressed oil	

Steam vegetables until just tender, drain and toss with oil and spice.

Serve with crispy chow mein noodles or with other boiled, or boiled and fried, noodles.

Place on a large serving platter with vegetables at the centre and keep hot while preparing omelettes.

Egg Foo Yung

1 cup mung bean sprouts	8 eggs
½ cup peas	herb salt
1 stick celery, angle-sliced	freshly ground pepper
1 medium onion, thinly sliced	cold-pressed oil

Combine vegetables in a bowl. Lightly beat eggs, salt and pepper in a separate bowl.

Heat oil, ensuring that it is at a depth of at least 3cm, over a medium heat (180°C on a thermometer). Lightly stir the vegetables into the eggs and using ¼ cup batter per omelette, cook 3 at a time, keeping oil hot. Turn after 30 seconds and fry for a further 30 seconds until puffy and golden. Serve at once.

• *Avocados Rancheros with Tofu or Eggs* •
• *Corn on the Cob or Steamed Beets* •
• *Pita Bread or Corn Chips* •

A particularly fast meal of Latin American origins. Traditionally Huevos Rancheros — ranch-style eggs — are served on a tortilla (a thin cornmeal "pancake"), surrounded by hot sauce and avocado. Here avocado halves are topped with eggs or grilled tofu and hot sauce.

Preparation Plan
- prepare sauce, tofu or eggs, and avocado
- cook corn or beets
- set out bread or chips, and serve

Avocados Rancheros

Hot Sauce:
cold-pressed oil
1 cup chopped onions
1 large green pepper, chopped
1-3 hot chillies
1-3 cloves garlic
5 medium tomatoes, chopped
¼ cup chopped parsley
1 tbs oreganum
2 tsp coriander

1 tsp brown sugar
herb salt

Tofu or Eggs:
2 blocks tofu or 4 eggs
natural soy sauce

Base:
2 large ripe avocados
lettuce

Fry the onion, pepper and garlic in oil over a medium heat until softened but not brown. Stir in remaining ingredients and bring to the boil. Simmer, partly covered, for about 15 minutes. Taste for seasoning.

Slice tofu into one large slab per person. Sprinkle with soy sauce and grill briefly on both sides until crisply coated. Or poach or fry eggs.

Slice each avocado in half. Remove stone and peel off skin. Cover each half with the hot tofu or egg and drape with sauce. Serve immediately on a bed of shredded lettuce.

Corn or Beets

4 corn on the cob or 4 beetroot, sliced

Meanwhile steam corn or beets for 10-15 minutes until tender.

Pita Bread or Corn Chips

pita bread or corn chips

Arrange and serve.

53   *Japanese Dinner #1*   SERVES 4-6

- *Umewan — clear soup with garnishes* •
- *Sushi — vinegared rice* •
- *Horenso Hitashik — sesame spinach* •

A few inexpensive specialty ingredients — available from many health food stores, delis, and Asian specialty shops — exotically flavour and authenticate your meal. Many Japanese dishes are quick to prepare with an emphasis on lightness, simplicity and ingenious elegance. Shrimp are traditionally a part of the soup, but scallops will be fresher, easier to obtain and, at one per person, affordable.

Preparation Plan
- cook rice; season once cooked
- prepare soup and garnishes
- prepare spinach, and serve

Sushi

2 cups brown rice	¼ cup rice vinegar or
3cm square kombu (dried kelp)	mild white vinegar
3¾ cups water	1 tsp herb salt
Dressing:	2 tbs sweet sake or
3½ tbs sugar	dry sherry

Bring the rice, water and kombu to the boil, and boil covered for 10 minutes.

Meanwhile prepare the Dressing: Bring all ingredients to the boil, uncovered, then remove from heat and allow to cool if there is time.

Once rice has boiled for 10 minutes, without uncovering turn heat off and cover top and sides of pan with a thick towel to trap in heat. Allow to sit undisturbed for 20 minutes or longer.

Transfer rice to a non-metallic serving dish and immediately pour on dressing and mix with a fork. (Traditionally this is served at room temperature and may be prepared well in advance.)

Umewan

6 cups water	4 eggs
2 x 4cm squares of kombu (dried kelp)	herb salt
1 cup katsuobushi (dried bonito) or ½ cup	
tinned tuna (a very rough exchange!)	200g fish fillets
3 large shiitake (dried Japanese	4-6 scallops
mushrooms)	5 tbs arrowroot or cornstarch
1 tbs soy sauce	herb salt
1 tbs Japanese rice wine or sherry	
1 tsp sugar	12 small sprigs watercress or parsley
	1 small carrot, grated
1 tbs cold-pressed oil	twists of lemon

While rice is steaming prepare soup. Bring water, kombu, bonito or tuna, shiitake, soy sauce, rice wine or sherry and sugar to the boil. Simmer for 15 minutes, then strain through a fine sieve. Return to the saucepan.

Meanwhile heat the oil over a medium heat until a drop of water flicked into it evaporates instantly. Beat the eggs and dash of herb salt until well combined. Pour about ¼ cup of the eggs into the pan and tip it to cover. Cook until the eggs coagulate into a thin film. Remove the omelette and roll it into a tight, thin cylinder. Repeat with remaining mixture.

Bring strained broth back to the boil. Meanwhile sprinkle the fish and scallops with salt. Dip in arrowroot or cornstarch and shake off excess. Add fish and scallops to the boiling broth and boil for 4 minutes. Remove with a slotted spoon and set aside. Turn broth to simmer and keep hot while readying garnishes.

In each soup bowl place 3 slices of omelette, one slice of fish, one scallop, 2 sprigs watercress or parsley, half a mushroom, and a few strips of carrot. Fill each bowl carefully with the broth, pouring it down the side of the bowl so as to least disturb the arrangement. Garnish with a twist of lemon.

Horenso Hitashi

½ kg spinach leaves and stems	¼ cup of Umewan broth
	1 tbs natural soy sauce
2 tbs sesame seeds	1 tsp sugar

Steam the spinach (do not chop) for about 5 minutes until it just begins to wilt. Immediately drain and plunge in cold water to set colour and stop cooking. Discard stems and squeeze leaves as dry as possible. Chop into 3cm pieces.

Toast the sesame seeds. Combine them with the broth, soy sauce and sugar. Pour over the spinach and toss. Sprinkle with the toasted sesame seeds.

- *Su Udon — noodles and chicken, or fish or tofu in broth* •
- *Nasu Karashi Sumiso-ae — eggplant in mustard dressing* •
- *Satsuma-Imo Amani — lemon sweet potato* •

Japanese meals tend to be an array of many small dishes rather than one main dish and lesser accompaniments. The noodle and broth dish can be served in individual deep bowls with the other dishes eaten alongside or afterwards. There is a basic dressing which is made and used as a base for the eggplant. Left-over dressing can be stored at room temperature or refrigerated for several months, and used as an all-purpose seasoning.

Preparation Plan
- prepare dressing and eggplant salad
- prepare lemon sweet potatoes
- prepare noodle dish, and serve

Nasu Karashi Sumiso-ae

1 tbs powdered mustard mixed with a little hot water to make a thick paste	3 tbs rice vinegar or other mild white vinegar 1 tbs natural soy sauce
300g eggplant	Miso Dressing:
300g green beans	½ cup miso
1 tsp seasalt	¼ cup sake (rice wine) or dry sherry
6-8 spring onions	¼ cup sugar
⅓ cup Miso Dressing	1 egg yolk

Combine mustard and water and set aside for 15 minutes.

Slice the eggplant into 5cm cubes; slice the beans and spring onions into 5cm lengths. Bring 2 cups water to the boil; add the vegetables and return to the boil. Boil for 3-5 minutes until the vegetables are tender. Drain at once and set aside.

Combine the vinegar and soy sauce with the Miso Dressing and mustard mixture. Toss with the vegetables until thoroughly coated. Serve at room temperature.

Satsuma-Imo Amani

450g sweet potatoes, preferably long and thin	3 tbs sugar dash salt
1 medium lemon	2½ cups water

Slice the sweet potatoes into 3cm thick slices. Slice lemon crosswise into 3cm thick slices. Bring these to the boil along with the sugar, salt and water. Cover, reduce heat and simmer until tender, for about 15 minutes. Drain and serve hot or at room temperature.

Su Udon

wide or spaghetti-type noodles; wheat, rice or buckwheat-based	½ cup sliced mushrooms or 6 sliced shiitake (dried Japanese mushrooms)
300g chicken breast, fish, or tofu sliced into narrow strips about 5cm long	2 tbs natural soy sauce
4 cups water	2 tbs sugar
1 small capsicum cut into thin strips	3cm kombu (dried kelp), broken into pieces

In a large saucepan bring to the boil all the ingredients. Cover and simmer for 10-15 minutes. Taste for seasoning and serve.

- *Teriyaki — grilled and glazed chicken or fish or tofu or beef* •
- *Kaki Age — tempura-style vegetable pancakes* •
- *Namasu — grated turnip and radish salad* •

The teriyaki sauce — which grills to a succulent glaze — can be stored in the fridge and used as an all-purpose seasoning. The tempura-style batter for the pancakes will be thinnish and should wait no longer than 10 minutes before cooking.

Preparation Plan
- marinate teriyaki choice; grill just before serving
- prepare pancakes and fry
- prepare salad, and serve

Teriyaki

one of the following protein options:
   small chicken legs or drumsticks
   fish fillets
   beef slices
   tofu slices

Teriyaki Sauce:
½ cup chicken or Vegetable Stock

½ cup natural soy sauce
½ cup mirin (sweet sake) or
   dry sherry

Teriyaki Glaze:
¼ cup Teriyaki Sauce
1 tbs sugar
2 tsp cornstarch or arrowroot

Bring the soy sauce, stock and mirin or option to the boil. Remove from heat and cool to room temperature. Reserve ¼ cup for the Glaze. Marinate the chicken or option in the Sauce. Combine Glaze ingredients in a small saucepan and bring almost to the boil. Reduce heat to low and stir constantly until a syrupy glaze forms.

Fifteen to thirty minutes before serving (depending on size and choice of protein used) heat grill on high and grill chicken or option for 5-10 minutes on one side until a rich golden brown. Dip again in marinade and grill on the other side. Place on a heated serving dish and coat with Glaze.

Kaki Age

Tempura-style Batter:
⅘ cup flour
⅔ cup ice water
1 egg yolk
¼ tsp seasalt
⅛ tsp baking soda

2 medium sweet potatoes, grated
½ cup green peas
½ cup corn
2 tbs grated ginger root
cooking oil

Beat the batter ingredients thoroughly, then stir in the vegetables and ginger. Heat the oil in a wok or frypan until very hot (190°C). Fry pancake mixture in about 2 tablespoon amounts for about one minute on each side. Drain on paper towels and keep warm while frying the remainder.

Namasu

200g turnip, peeled and grated
6 large radishes, grated
1 small carrot, grated

2 tbs seaweed
2 tbs rice vinegar
2 tsp sugar
herb salt

Briefly soak seaweed in water; drain and chop. Combine the seaweed, vinegar, sugar and salt. Stir in the grated vegetables. Serve at room temperature.

- *Ginger Potatoes* •
- *Scrambled Eggs and Broccoli* •
- *Cucumber Rayta* •

Indian meals are simple and quick, imaginatively glorify vegetables, need not be firey hot, and are vastly more diverse than the curry-powder-sauce-coated food familiar to many. The Rayta dish mentioned refers to a yoghurt-based salad.

Preparation Plan
- prepare potatoes
- prepare rayta and chill
- prepare egg dish, and serve

Ginger Potatoes

¼ cup ghee or oil
1 tbs finely chopped garlic
1 tbs finely chopped ginger
½ cup finely chopped onion
herb salt
2 tsp cumin
½ tsp turmeric

¼ tsp chilli powder
4 medium tomatoes, chopped
4 potatoes, cubed
1 cup peas
1 cup water
1 tsp garam masala

In ghee or oil fry the ginger, garlic, onions and salt until tender. Add seasonings and tomatoes and cook for 5 minutes until thick.

Add the peas, potatoes and water and bring to the boil. Cover and simmer for 10 minutes until tender. Sprinkle with garam masala and serve.

Cucumber Rayta

1 cup yoghurt or Savoury Tofu Whip
1 medium cucumber, peeled and cubed

2 tsp coriander
3 tbs chopped fresh mint

Combine all the ingredients and chill until serving time.

Scrambled Eggs and Broccoli

ghee or oil
2 cups small cauliflower pieces
1 tsp finely chopped ginger root
6 eggs
¼ cup milk (cow, goat, soy, coconut cream)
1 or more chopped fresh chillies

herb salt
2 spring onions, chopped
3 tbs chopped parsley
1 tsp cumin
¼ tsp turmeric

In the ghee or oil cook broccoli and ginger until crisply tender. Meanwhile lightly beat the eggs, then stir in the remaining ingredients. Reduce the heat to low and, stirring constantly, cook the eggs until creamy curds form. Do not overcook. Serve immediately.

Indian Dinner #2 SERVES 4

- • *Beetroot Salad* •
- • *Spinach and Dahl Puree* •
- • *Black Mustard Cauliflower* •

If you wish to shorten cooking time, soak the dahl (yellow lentils) overnight or in the morning. The various seeds add authentic flavour. The salad is best with ample marination time.

Preparation Plan
- • marinate salad
- • cook dahl and spinach
- • prepare cauliflower, and serve

Beetroot Salad

1 large scrubbed beetroot, very thinly sliced
1 large onion, thinly sliced
2 medium tomatoes, sliced
1 fresh green chilli, chopped

3 tbs cold-pressed oil
2 tbs lemon juice
2 tbs chopped fresh mint
herb salt

Layer the vegetables and chilli pepper in a narrow-based salad bowl. Combine the remaining ingredients, pour over top, and cover. Marinate at room temperature for 30 minutes, or one hour or more if refrigerated.

Spinach and Dahl Puree

1¼ cups dahl or yellow lentils
3 cups water
herb salt

1 cup water
250g spinach, chopped
250g broccoli, chopped

3 tbs ghee or oil
1 tbs finely chopped ginger root
1 tbs finely chopped garlic
herb salt
1 tsp cumin powder
1 tsp coriander
1 tsp garam masala

Bring dahl, water and salt to the boil, and boil, partly covered, until tender, for 20-30 minutes. Drain thoroughly.

Puree the spinach, broccoli and water in batches in the blender until smoothly pureed.

Heat the ghee or oil over a medium heat and fry the garlic, ginger and spices for 2 minutes. Stir in the puree, about a cup at a time, and fry for 5 minutes more. Simmer uncovered for 10 minutes until thick. Stir in dahl and cook for 5 minutes or longer.

Black Mustard Cauliflower

3 tbs cold-pressed oil
½ cup peanuts
½ tsp black mustard seeds
½ tsp cumin seeds

½ tsp turmeric
herb salt
1 head cauliflower, in small-medium pieces
2 tsp honey

Heat the oil over a moderate heat and add the seeds and peanuts. Cook, stirring constantly, for one minute, then add the salt and turmeric and cook for another 3 minutes. Stir in the cauliflower pieces and the honey and reduce the heat to low. Cook until just tender.

- *Lentil Balls* •
- *Yoghurt or Tofu Sauce* •
- *Lemon and Ginger Salad* •

The lentils require two hours advance soaking which can be accomplished in the morning if that's easier. When the balls are frying remember not to overcrowd as they puff up to twice their original size.

Preparation Plan
- soak lentils; marinate salad
- prepare lentil balls and fry
- prepare sauce, and serve

Lemon and Ginger Salad

1 lemon, halved and thinly sliced	3 tbs lemon juice
2 medium tomatoes, sliced	1 tbs grated ginger root
½ small cucumber, peeled and sliced	herb salt

Combine all the ingredients in a salad bowl. Cover and chill, stirring occasionally.

Lentil Balls

1 cup dahl or lentils	1 tbs finely chopped green chilli pepper
2 cups cold water	2 tsp coriander
	1 tsp finely chopped garlic
1 cup finely chopped fresh coriander	herb salt
or parsley	oil

In the morning, soak the lentils in the water at room temperature for 2 hours or longer.

In the evening, combine the lentils and their water and the remaining ingredients in a blender and whizz until smoothly pureed.

Heat one cup or more oil in a frypan or wok until very hot (180°C). For each ball drop about a tablespoon of lentil mixture into the hot oil. Fry 5 or 6 balls at a time, about 3 minutes on each side until golden brown all over. Drain on paper towels and keep hot in a warm oven while preparing succeeding batches.

Yoghurt or Tofu Sauce

1½ cups yoghurt or Savoury Tofu Whip	2 tsp cumin powder
½ cup coconut	herb salt

Combine all the ingredients and serve at room temperature.

Indian Dinner #4

- *Spiced and Nutty Saffron Rice* •
- *Tamarillo Chutney* •
- *Coconut Chips* •

The line between a salad and a true Indian chutney is a fine one. Traditionally chutneys are prepared fresh each day and may be raw or cooked. The saffron required in the rice gives a specific flavour but it is expensive — turmeric is a cheaper alternative.

Preparation Plan
- cook rice
- prepare chutney
- set out chips, and serve

Spiced and Nutty Saffron Rice

1 tsp saffron threads, soaked in 3 tbs boiling water for 10 minutes or ½ tsp turmeric	1 tsp finely chopped garlic
6 tbs ghee or oil	1 tsp cumin seeds
1 cup finely chopped onions	½ tsp nutmeg
1 cup mixed nuts	1-2 tsp herb salt
1 tbs grated ginger root	2 cups brown rice
4 peppercorns	3¾ cups boiling water
4 cloves	1 cup chopped green beans
5cm stick cinnamon	1 tbs molasses
	1 tbs brown sugar

Heat the ghee or oil over a medium heat until very hot and add onions, nuts and seasonings (as a time-saving device get the onions cooking first and add the remaining ingredients as you ready them). Fry for 5 minutes, stirring constantly until the onions are soft.

Stir in the rice and the remaining ingredients including the saffron and water or the turmeric, and bring to the boil. Boil for 10 minutes, covered and without lifting the lid, turn off the heat and cover the top and sides of the saucepan with a thick towel to trap in the heat. Leave undisturbed for 20 minutes or more.

Tamarillo Chutney

3 tamarillos, peeled and diced	¼ cup dates, chopped
2 medium carrots, grated	¼ cup lemon juice
1 small capsicum, diced	1 tsp cumin powder
3 radishes, diced	

Combine all the ingredients, cover and chill until serving time, stirring occasionally.

Banana Chips

purchased banana chips

Place in 2 small bowls at either end of the table and use to sprinkle on rice.

• *Dosa Breads* •
• *Eggplant Rayta* •
• *Toasted Coconut Vegetables* •

Dosa are flat pan-cooked breads made from ground lentils and rice. They can be used as a scoop to eat the other dishes with. Be prepared for the several aspects of day-before soaking and mixing.

Preparation Plan
- soak dosa batter; puree and let sit; cook
- grill eggplant; chop, toss and chill
- cook vegetables, and serve

Dosa

½ cup split peas or lentils	or parsley
1½ cups brown rice	2 tbs grated ginger root
	1 fresh green chilli, finely chopped (optional)
½ cup finely chopped onions	herb salt
¼ cup finely chopped fresh coriander	3 tbs ghee or oil

In the afternoon of the previous day: soak the legumes and rice in about 4 cups water at room temperature for 3 hours or more. Then, in the evening, drain the legumes and rice and puree in batches in a blender with a total of 1 cup fresh water. Cover the batter tightly and let sit at room temperature for at least 12 hours.

Before cooking stir in the remaining ingredients. Heat ½ tsp ghee or oil over a moderate heat until a drop of water flicked in splutters instantly. Pour in ½ cup of the batter and tip pan to spread evenly. Fry for 2-3 minutes until bubbles form on top. Drizzle with another ½ tsp of ghee and turn over. Cook for 2 minutes more until well browned. Serve warm or at room temperature.

Eggplant Rayta

1 large (½ kg) eggplant	3 tbs fresh mint, chopped
cold-pressed oil	2 tsp coriander
1 cup yoghurt or Savoury Tofu Whip	herb salt
3 tomatoes, chopped	

While dosa are cooking slice eggplant into 10mm slices and brush with oil. Grill for about 5 minutes on each side. Chop coarsely and toss with remaining ingredients. Chill.

Toasted Coconut Vegetables

3 tbs cold-pressed oil	2 medium potatoes, diced
1 tsp black mustard seeds	2 large carrots, diced
1 tsp cumin seeds	3 courgettes, sliced
¾ cup coconut	herb salt

While dosa are cooking and after preparing rayta, fry the seeds in oil over a moderate heat for 3 minutes. Add coconut and potatoes and cook for about 5 minutes until coconut is coloured — stir frequently. Add the remaining vegetables and ½ cup water. Bring to the boil and then simmer for 10 minutes or more. Add herb salt and taste for seasoning.

---

61   *Country Cottage Pie*   SERVES 4-5

- *Vegetable Cottage Pie* •
- *Tomatoes in Vinaigrette* •

A one-dish dinner of three scrumptious homey layers: stewed vegetables in an aromatic gravy; lemon-scented mashed pumpkin or potato; and a crispy pumpkin kernel topping. The marinated tomatoes are a fresh, moist accompaniment.

Preparation Plan
- steam pumpkin or potato; stew vegetables
- mash pumpkin; prepare topping; layer; grill
- marinate tomatoes, and serve

Vegetable Cottage Pie

Potato/Pumpkin Layer:
3 cups cubed, unpeeled pumpkin
  or potato
3 beaten eggs
grated rind and juice of 1 lemon
3 tbs butter or oil
3 spring onions, chopped
herb salt

Stewed Vegetables:
3-4 cups mixed vegetables such as
  cauliflower, peas, carrot
3 cups Vegetable Stock

¼ cup and 2 tbs rice flour
3 tsp miso or marmite
2 tsp food yeast
1 tsp of each:
  tarragon
  mixed herbs
  paprika
½ tsp cardamom or garam masala
¼ tsp sage

Crispy Pumpkin Topping:
⅔ cup pumpkin kernels
2 tbs natural soy sauce

Steam pumpkin or potato for about 5 minutes until soft. Mash, then blend in the remaining ingredients. (While steaming prepare the Stewed Vegetables.)

Bring all the stew ingredients to the boil, then simmer for 15 minutes or longer until tender and flavourful. Taste for seasoning.

While simmering prepare Crispy Pumpkin Topping and the Tomatoes in Vinaigrette.

Place Stewed Vegetables in a deep, oiled 25cm casserole dish and cover with the mashed pumpkin. (Remember to keep each layer hot before final assembly.)

Combine the pumpkin kernels and the soy sauce. Sprinkle over vegetables. Place the pie under a grill to brown and crispen for a few minutes. Watch carefully!

Tomatoes In Vinaigrette

3-5 tomatoes, sliced
2 tbs olive oil
1-2 tsp food yeast (optional)

½ tsp dill seed
herb salt

Combine all the ingredients. Cover and allow to marinate, chilled or at room temperature.

- *Pumpkin-Crusted Peanut Pie* •
- *Soy Salad* •

Really just a variation on Country Cottage Pie, this time with the mashed vegetable layer (carrot or sweet potato would also work well) as the crust rather than as the topping. Once you see the principle at work many variations are possible.

Preparation Plan
- steam and mash pumpkin and use as crust
- prepare filling; assemble and bake
- prepare salad, and serve

Pumpkin-Crusted Peanut Pie

Crust:
chopped pumpkin to make about
  2 cups mashed
¼ cup rice flour or other
1 tsp curry powder
½ tsp bouquet garni
¼ tsp nutmeg
herb salt

Filling:
2 cups small cauliflower pieces
1 cup chopped cabbage
2 cups Vegetable Stock

3 tbs peanut butter
3 tbs rice flour or other
2 tbs natural soy sauce
1 tbs apple cider vinegar
1 tbs honey
1 tsp paprika
1 tsp Chinese 5-spice
1 tsp powdered ginger
¼ tsp allspice
3cm peeled ginger root, diced

¾ cup toasted peanuts

Steam pumpkin until tender, then mash. Meanwhile prepare Filling.

Bring all the Filling ingredients except peanuts to a rolling boil. Simmer for a few minutes while preparing crust. Preheat oven to 200ºC.

Add flour and seasonings to mashed pumpkin and pat into an oiled 23cm pie plate. Stir peanuts into filling and pour it into pie crust.

Bake for 15-20 minutes until set. If possible let it sit out of the oven for 5-10 minutes for easier slicing.

Soy Salad

2 tbs cold-pressed oil
1 block tofu, cubed
2 tbs natural soy sauce
cucumber, cubed

spinach leaves, torn
tomatoes, chopped
2 tbs cold-pressed oil
1 tsp cumin powder

In 2 tablespoons oil fry the tofu until well crisped. Sprinkle with soy sauce. Toss with remaining ingredients; and serve.

- *Sesame Onion Pie* •
- *Kumara (Sweet Potato) Slices* •
- *Mixed Greens* •

This pie recipe is an old favourite from a scrapbook I started as a child: which should only reinforce how simple it is to prepare.

Preparation Plan
- saute onion; prepare crust; assemble and bake
- slice and bake kumara
- steam greens, and serve

Sesame Onion Pie

2 tbs butter or margarine	¾ cup milk (cow, goat, soy, coconut cream)
2 cups thinly sliced onions	½ tsp thyme
	¼ tsp nutmeg
1 cup fine cracker crumbs	¼ cup shredded tasty cheese or
¼ cup melted butter or margarine	crumbled feta (cow, goat, sheep)
	sesame seeds
2 eggs	paprika

In butter or option slowly fry the onions for about 10 minutes until tender — do not brown. Meanwhile preheat oven to 180ºC. Combine cracker crumbs and melted butter, and press into a 20cm pie plate.

Beat together the eggs, milk, thyme and nutmeg. Place the onions in the pie shell and cover with cheese. Cover with milk mixture. Sprinkle with sesame seeds and paprika. Bake for 20-30 minutes until a knife inserted in the centre comes out dry.

Kumara (Sweet Potato) Slices

kumara	oil

Slice kumara thinly. Place as vertically as possible in an oiled pan in one layer and brush lightly with oil. Bake beside the pie until tender — about 25 minutes.

Mixed Greens

silverbeet, coarsely torn	celery, angle-cut
broccoli, medium-large segments	brussels sprouts, halved

Steam all the vegetables together until tender. Drain and serve.

Eggplant Pie

- *Eggplant Pie* •
- *Pasta or Potatoes Brazil* •
- *Celery and Courgette Stix* •

A moist Mediterranean-style casserole-pie with layers of eggplant, tomato and yoghurt or tofu. Of course many adaptations and additions are possible by using rice, noodles, starchy vegetables, meat, fish, pinenuts, etc.

Preparation Plan
- prepare pie
- prepare pasta or potatoes
- prepare stix, and serve

Eggplant Pie

2-3 large eggplant	1½ cups yoghurt or
olive oil	Savoury Tofu Whip
2-4 cloves garlic, chopped	1 tbs oreganum
1 medium onion, sliced	2 tsp basil
1½ cups chopped tomatoes	herb salt

Slice eggplant at short end into 10mm slices. Brush thoroughly with olive oil. Grill both sides until limp and dark.

Meanwhile fry remaining vegetables in olive oil until cooked to a thick pulp — about 10 minutes. Preheat oven to 200°C.

In an oiled, deep 20-23cm casserole dish layer eggplant slices, tomato pulp and yoghurt or option, sprinkling with herbs and salt as you layer. Cover with foil and bake for 20 minutes or longer.

Pasta or Potatoes Brazil

pasta or potatoes	1 green pepper, sliced
3 tbs cold-pressed oil	2 tsp coriander
½-¾ cup chopped brazils	½ tsp turmeric
1 cup chopped cabbage	herb salt

Cook pasta according to packet instructions. (For rice-noodles see Cook's Tips.) Drain. Or steam sliced potatoes until tender.

Meanwhile fry the remaining ingredients over a medium heat until crispy tender. Toss with pasta or potatoes.

Celery and Courgette Stix

celery	courgettes

Slice the vegetables into sticks and serve.

---

65   *Tomato Rice Pie*   *SERVES 4-6*

- *Tomato Rice Pie* •
- *Baby Scallopini* •
- *Beet and Celery Salad* •

A good summertime dish when tomatoes are plentiful, though this recipe lends itself to an array of filling and crust options. Try a salmon and yoghurt filling with a mashed potato crust; or an eggplant, salami or cheese and capsicum filling with a mashed pumpkin or carrot crust. Left over (unsweetened) breakfast cereal can also be mixed with flour, oil and herbs and used as a crust. The rice needs only 10 minutes of your presence in the morning say, to cook.

Preparation Plan
- cook rice; prepare crust and filling; bake
- steam vegetables
- prepare salad, and serve

Tomato Rice Pie

Crust:
¾ cup brown rice
1½ cups water
½ green pepper, finely chopped
herb salt
¼ tsp turmeric
3 tbs cold-pressed oil

7-8 medium-sized firm tomatoes

Filling:
1½ cups grated cheese or
    grated or crumbled tofu
8 chopped olives
¼ cup chopped parsley
¼ cup chopped spring onions
2 tsp oreganum
2 tsp basil
herb salt

In the morning, bring all the crust ingredients (except oil) to the boil, covered, and boil for 10 minutes. Without removing lid, turn off heat, and let sit undisturbed for 20 minutes or more, covering the top and sides of the pan with a thick towel to trap in heat.

In the evening preheat oven to 200°C. Combine the rice with 3 tablespoons oil and press into a 23cm pie plate as for a crust.

Slice the tomatoes into 10mm slices. Combine remaining ingredients. On pie crust layer: tomatoes, tofu mixture, tomatoes, tofu mixture, tomatoes.

Bake for 20 minutes or more until very hot and bubbly. For a better slicing pie let sit for 5-10 minutes before slicing.

Baby Scallopini
baby scallopini or other green vegetable

Steam until tender and serve.

Beet and Celery Salad
grated beetroot
celery sticks

3 tbs yoghurt or Homemade Mayonnaise
1 tsp curry powder

Place grated beetroot in a shallow bowl and stud its outside edge with celery sticks. Combine remaining ingredients and drizzle over beetroot.

Carrot Soufflé

- *Carrot Soufflé* -
- *Noodles aux Fine Herbes* -
- *Celery Salad* -

A soufflé in 40 minutes? Mais oui!

Preparation Plan
- prepare and bake soufflé
- prepare noodles
- prepare salad, and serve

Carrot Soufflé

4 cups grated carrot
1½ cups yoghurt or coconut cream
6 eggs
¼ cup grated parmesan or
    ground, toasted sunflower seed kernels
¼ cup finely chopped spring onions
¼ cup flour

3 tbs butter or oil
1 tsp dill seed
1 tsp tarragon
1 tsp basil
1 tsp oreganum
½ tsp nutmeg
herb salt

Preheat oven to 200°C. Beat egg yolks until very thick. Beat in all the ingredients — except carrot — until well combined. Stir in carrot.

Beat egg whites until very stiff. Fold into carrot mixture gently but thoroughly. Grease the bottom only of a 2-litre soufflé dish and pour in mixture. Place on the middle rack of the oven, then immediately turn heat to 190°C. Bake for 25-30 minutes until soufflé puffs up about 5cm above the rim and the top is lightly browned. Serve at once.

Noodles aux Fine Herbes

shell-shaped or other wheat,
    buckwheat or rice-noodles
¼ cup finely chopped spinach
2 tbs cold-pressed oil
2 tbs finely chopped parsley

2 tbs finely chopped dill
1 tsp oreganum
1 tsp basil
herb salt

Cook pasta according to packet instructions. (For rice-noodles see Cook's Tips.) Drain and toss with the remaining ingredients.

Celery Salad

celery, sliced
cucumber, peeled and cubed
red pepper, sliced

2 tbs cold-pressed oil
2 tbs lemon juice
1 tsp paprika

Combine the oil and lemon juice with paprika. Toss with the vegetables to thoroughly combine.

- *Fish Roe Soufflé* •
- *Kumara (Sweet Potato) Crisps* •
- *Harvest Salad* •

With the price of fish these days, learning to use cheaper fishy alternatives is a must. Instead of the fish roe in the soufflé try smoked fish, tinned fish or chopped mussels.

Preparation Plan
- prepare and bake soufflé
- bake kumara
- prepare salad, and serve

Fish Roe Soufflé

5 large eggs, separated	2 tbs finely chopped onion
1 cup fish roe, chopped	2 tbs finely chopped red pepper
(or option as above)	1½ cups corn
5 tbs rice flour or other	1 tsp bouquet garni
3 tbs melted butter or oil	herb salt

If you have a self-standing electric beater, beat egg whites until stiff while preparing the remaining ingredients. If beating by hand, prepare the other ingredients first. Preheat oven to 200°C.

Thoroughly beat the egg yolks until thick. Beat in other ingredients, except the corn. Then stir in the corn.

Stir in about 3 tablespoons of beaten egg white, then gently fold in remainder. Pour into a soufflé dish (only grease the bottom of the dish) and bake for 30 minutes or more until puffed and lightly brown on top. Serve at once.

Kumara (Sweet Potato) Crisps

kumara	oreganum
paprika	cold-pressed oil

Oil a shallow baking dish. Very thinly slice the kumara and place — as upright as possible — in the dish. Drizzle with oil and sprinkle with seasonings.

Bake with the soufflé for about 20 minutes or more until crisp.

Harvest Salad

grated beetroot	lemon juice
lettuce, shredded	curry powder
courgettes, grated	basil

On a serving platter arrange an outer circle of lettuce, then an inner circle of beetroot, and a centrepiece of courgette. Drizzle generously with lemon juice and sprinkle with seasonings.

- *Antipasto* -
- *Pizza Paisano with choice of crusts and toppings* -

A fun peasanty people-pleaser. Start off with your antipasto (a salad platter in disguise) as a first course. If social standards permit, serve it with a side bowl of mayonnaise mixed with lots of raw garlic to dip your crunchy vegetables in. For further time-saving have your first course while the pizza bakes.

Preparation Plan
- prepare and bake pizza
- prepare antipasto, and serve

Pizza Paisano

Crust:
crumbled gluten-free cornbread or
    4 large wholemeal pita breads

Italian Tomato Sauce:
3 cups chopped tomatoes
2½ tbs marmite or miso
2 tbs olive oil

1 tbs apple cider vinegar
2 tsp brown sugar
½ small onion
4 cloves garlic
2 tsp basil
2 tsp oreganum
¼ tsp nutmeg

For cornbread crust crumble bread into a large oiled pizza pan or baking pan. Put in oven or under grill briefly to toast and firm while making sauce. For pita crust simply place the breads in a single layer on baking pans or trays.

Whizz all the ingredients in a blender. Pour into a saucepan. Bring to the boil and simmer for 10 minutes or longer until rich, dark and flavourful. Taste for seasoning. Preheat oven to 250°C.

Prepare choice of topping ingredients, then top crust with sauce, then topping ingredients in order given. Sprinkle with more oreganum and basil and bake for 15-20 minutes until well crisped.

Toppings

VEGETARIAN:	MARINARA:	MEAT:
crumbled tofu and/or grated cheese	grated cheese	grated cheese
olives	vegetables (as for Vegetarian Topping)	vegetables (as for Vegetarian Topping)
mushrooms	one or more of the following:	one or more of the following:
green pepper	mussels	salami
courgette	oysters	bacon
drizzle of olive oil	squid	ham
	anchovies	spicy sausage, sliced
	salmon or tuna	mince
	sardines	left-over cooked meat

Antipasto

lettuce leaves

carrot sticks

cauliflower segments

celery sticks

further options:

  anchovies

  olives

  marinated mussels

   or oysters

sardines

pickled onions

Dressing:

4 tbs olive oil

1 tbs lemon juice

1 tsp prepared mustard

1 tsp basil

herb salt to taste

On a large platter arrange a bed of lettuce leaves. Top with a selection of raw vegetables and any options desired. Drizzle generously with the dressing and sprinkle with freshly ground black pepper.

In addition the platter may be accompanied with a mixture of Homemade Mayonnaise and garlic, as outlined above.

Combine all the dressing ingredients and taste for seasoning.

---

69 *Transylvanian Casserole* SERVES 4-6

- *Transylvanian Cabbage Casserole* •
- *Mushroom Salad* •

Honestly there is a Transylvania (a region of Rumania) and this is one of its specialties. The dish is ideal prepared with a spicy sausage but toasted nuts and seeds make a crunchy flavourful option. Sauerkraut is pickled cabbage.

Preparation Plan
- cook rice; prepare vegetables; layer and bake
- prepare salad, and serve

Transylvanian Cabbage Casserole

2 cups brown rice
1¾ cups water or Vegetable Stock
2 cups coconut cream or mixture of
  1½ cups sour cream and ½ cup milk

2 tbs paprika
1 cup chopped spicy sausage or
  ¾ cup mixed peanuts and sunflower
  seed kernels

3 tbs butter or oil
1 cup finely chopped onions
1 tsp finely chopped garlic

450g sauerkraut
1 cup Vegetable Stock

Grind the rice in a blender to roughly crack. Bring to the boil with the water, covered, and boil for 5 minutes. Add cream or option, cover and bring to the boil; then without uncovering, turn off the heat and allow to sit for 5 minutes or longer while preparing other ingredients.

In the butter or oil slowly fry the onion, garlic and paprika until tender. Fry in the sausage or option. Preheat oven to 200ºC. Oil a large, not-too-deep casserole dish. Fill with the sauerkraut.

Once the rice and vegetables are cooked, combine them and taste for seasoning. Pour on top of the sauerkraut. Cover with the 1 cup of Vegetable Stock and bake for 20 minutes or more, until bubbly and the top is crisp.

Mushroom Salad

2 tbs cold-pressed oil
2 tbs white wine vinegar
2 tbs chopped chives

½ tsp bouquet garni
sliced mushrooms
sliced tomatoes

Combine the dressing ingredients, then toss with vegetables and serve.

- *Sardinian Lasagne — Vegetarian or Fish or Meat* •
  • *Tossed Salad* •

A simple, economical meal with that innately satisfying presence that Italian cooking brings. Experiment with using other sauce recipes and vegetable combinations, and layering these with pasta, potato, fish, tofu, etc to create your own casserole ideas.

Preparation Plan
- cook noodles; prepare sauce
- preheat oven; slice tomatoes; layer and bake
- toss salad, and serve

Sardinian Lasagne

Pasta:
about 3 cups pasta: wholemeal, spinach, rice or buckwheat

Sauce:
3 cups Vegetable Stock
6 tbs rice flour or other
3 medium courgettes, diced
1 large onion, sliced
1 large green pepper, chopped
1 cup chopped broccoli
1 tbs miso or marmite
1 tbs oreganum
2 tsp basil

3 bay leaves
choice of protein option:
  2-3 tins sardines, drained
  1-2 tins tuna, drained
  smoked fish, flaked
  cubed tofu or tempeh
  salami, bacon, ham, mince or
    left-over cooked meat

Tomato Layer:
4-6 large tomatoes, sliced
¾ cup pinenuts
basil and oreganum
olive oil

Cook pasta according to packet instructions. For rice or buckwheat noodles: bring water to the boil; add noodles and return to the boil; turn off heat; cover and let sit for 5-8 minutes until barely tender.

While noodles are cooking prepare the sauce. Bring all the ingredients to the boil and simmer for 10 minutes or longer. Taste for seasoning.

Preheat the oven to 200ºC. Prepare the Tomato Layer ingredients.

In an oiled casserole dish layer: half the pasta, half the sauce, half the tomatoes and pinenuts. Sprinkle with basil and oreganum. Repeat layers as above. Drizzle top with olive oil.

Bake in the oven for 15-20 minutes until hot and bubbly.

Tossed Salad

spinach or lettuce
carrots, thinly sliced
cucumber, thinly sliced
olives

olive oil
basil
freshly ground black pepper

Toss the vegetables and drizzle with olive oil, basil and pepper.

● *Nutty Noodle Ring with Salad Garnish* ●
● *Saucy Vegetables* ●

A unique way of serving noodles. Cooked noodles are tossed with nuts and herbs and pressed into a ring mould. The mould is then baked au bain-marie (in a pan of hot water), then inverted onto a serving platter. Delightful and delicious. Remember this as an attractive side-dish when entertaining.

Preparation Plan
- prepare noodle ring
- prepare vegetables, and serve

Nutty Noodle Ring

300g packet noodles: wheat, spinach,
   rice or buckwheat
¾ cup chopped nuts
3 tbs butter or margarine
handful chopped parsley
1 tsp basil

1 tsp paprika
1 tsp or more herb salt

extra chopped nuts
grated carrot

Cook noodles according to packet instructions. (For rice-noodles see Cook's Tips.) Preheat oven to 190ºC.

Meanwhile toast the nuts. Remove from heat and stir in butter, herbs and salt.

Drain noodles and toss with nut mixture. Grease a 6-cup mould ring, and press in the noodles. Place mould in a pan of hot water 3cm deep. Bake for 20 minutes. Invert onto a warm serving platter and garnish with grated carrot and more chopped nuts.

Saucy Vegetables

2-3 cups mixed seasonal vegetables such as:
   brussels sprouts
   parsnip
   onion rings
   green beans
3 cups Vegetable Stock

6 tbs rice flour or other
3 tbs natural soy sauce
1 tsp diced, peeled ginger root
1 tsp curry powder
1 tsp mixed herbs
½ tsp nutmeg

Bring all the vegetables to the boil and simmer for 15 minutes or more.

Taste for seasoning.

72 *Spinach & Noodle Casserole* SERVES 4-6

- *Spinach and Noodle Casserole* •
- *Green Beans and Walnuts* •
- *Herbed Tomatoes* •

I'm not suggesting that you can serve these in rapid succession, but yes, this is another Ukrainian noodle casserole — obviously these people are nuts about noodles! I'm sure you can see the pattern to their construction, so you'll be able to formulate your own interesting variations.

Preparation Plan
- cook noodles and assemble casserole
- prepare beans
- prepare tomatoes, and serve

Spinach and Noodle Casserole

2-3 cups spaghetti noodles — wheat, buckwheat or rice-noodles
butter or margarine
1 cup finely chopped onions
1 tsp finely chopped garlic
½ cup sliced mushrooms
herb salt

4 cups finely chopped spinach
1 cup (200g) crumbled feta (cow, sheep, goat) or grated gruyere
extra sliced mushrooms
chopped black olives
2 tbs melted butter or margarine

Cook noodles according to packet directions. (For rice-noodles see Cook's Tips.) Drain. Meanwhile fry the onion, garlic and mushrooms in the butter until tender. Toss with the cooked noodles.

While noodles are cooking, chop the spinach and prepare other ingredients. Preheat oven to 200ºC.

In a greased 8-12 cup casserole dish layer the noodles, then spinach, cheese and repeat, ending with a third layer of noodles on top. Cover with mushrooms and olives and drizzle with melted butter. Bake for 20 minutes or more until crisp.

Green Beans and Walnuts

green beans
brussels sprouts
2 tbs cold-pressed oil

1 tsp paprika
1 tsp coriander
¼ cup chopped walnuts

Steam the vegetables just until tender. Drain and toss with the remaining ingredients.

Herbed Tomatoes

sliced tomatoes
3 tbs red wine vinegar

2 tbs chopped parsley
freshly ground black pepper

Combine all the ingredients and serve. This salad also suits being covered, chilled and allowed to marinate.

- *Cheese-y Noodle Casserole* •
- *Red Cabbage with Pineapple* •
- *Courgette Slices* •

Another Ukrainian (my grandfather's background) casserole similar in concept to Potato Babka. The red cabbage and cucumber are also traditional Slav accompaniments.

Preparation Plan
- cook noodles and assemble casserole
- cook cabbage
- prepare courgettes, and serve

Cheese-y Noodle Casserole

2-3 cups ribbon noodles — wheat, buckwheat or rice-noodles
2 tbs butter or oil
1 medium onion, chopped
¾ cup pumpkin kernels
herb salt

3 tbs butter or margarine
½ cup dry bread or cracker crumbs
2 cups cottage cheese or mashed tofu
2 eggs
½ cup cream or coconut cream
2 tsp curry powder

Cook the noodles according to packet directions. (For rice-noodles see Cook's Tips). Drain.

Fry the onion and kernels in butter or oil until onion is tender. Toss with the noodles and herb salt. Preheat oven to 200°C.

Melt butter, remove from heat and stir in breadcrumbs.

Combine cheese with eggs, cream and curry powder. If using tofu add salt to taste.

Oil a 6-8 cup casserole dish and fill with a layer of noodles; top with half the cheese mixture, noodles, cheese, noodles. Top with the breadcrumbs. Bake for 20 minutes or more until crumbs are golden brown. Serve at once.

Red Cabbage with Pineapple

sliced red cabbage
carrots, angle-sliced into 3cm segments
1 cup unsweetened crushed pineapple and juice

2 tbs natural soy sauce
2 tbs apple cider vinegar
2 tbs brown sugar
2 tbs rice flour

Steam cabbage and carrots until very lightly cooked. Drain. Combine remaining ingredients and pour into pot with the vegetables. Simmer for 5-10 minutes until thick and flavourful.

Courgette Slices

courgettes

Slice on an angle, arrange and serve.

74   *Smoked Fish Casserole*   *SERVES 4*

• *Potato and Smoked Fish Casserole* •
• *Herb Salad* •

This dish is based on "Laksloda", a northwest North American Indian dish made with smoked salmon. You could easily invent an alternative vegetarian filling like tofu and toasted peanuts or grated courgette and sunflower seed kernels. This is one of those helpful meals which gives you some extra work or relaxation time while the main dish is baking.

Preparation Plan
- steam potatoes; assemble and bake casserole
- prepare salad, and serve

Potato and Smoked Fish Casserole

4 medium potatoes, very thinly sliced	2 tsp basil
¼ cup finely chopped onions	2 cups coconut cream
¼ cup finely chopped parsley	½ tsp allspice
400g smoked fish	

Steam the potatoes for about 5 minutes until tender. Meanwhile preheat oven to 200ºC and prepare the remaining ingredients.

In a well-greased 6-cup casserole dish layer: a third of the potatoes, onion, parsley, fish and basil.

Repeat layers and top with remaining potatoes. Pour the cream over the top and sprinkle with allspice. Bake for 25-30 minutes until tender and bubbly.

Herb Salad

Dressing:	lettuce
4 tbs olive oil	chopped fresh mint
1 tbs apple cider vinegar	chopped fresh lemon balm
1 tbs mustard	chopped fresh chives
1 tsp honey	tomatoes, sliced
1 tsp paprika	cucumber, sliced
1 tsp basil	

Combine all the dressing ingredients in a salad bowl. Then toss with the vegetables and herbs.

75 *Greek Casserole*

- *Greek Casserole* •
- *Buckwheat Pilaf* •
- *Carrot Sticks* •

Like a lasagne without the noodles, this is a colourful and succulent mixture of a type thee Mediterranean people do so well. Tofu can be substituted for the cheese, and barley or rice for the buckwheat.

Preparation Plan
- grill eggplant, prepare sauce, layer and bake
- cook buckwheat
- prepare carrots, and serve

Greek Casserole

2 large eggplant	2 tsp coriander
olive oil	½ tsp cinnamon
6 large tomatoes, coarsely chopped	250g crumbled feta (goat, sheep) or
4 courgettes, sliced	other cheese
1 large green pepper, sliced	¼ cup chopped parsley
1 cup thinly sliced onions	2 tsp basil
1 tsp finely chopped garlic	

Slice eggplant into 10mm slices. Brush with olive oil and grill for a few minutes on each side until dark and cooked.

Meanwhile prepare vegetables and sauce: in olive oil fry vegetables and spices until tender. Stir in cheese, parsley and basil; remove from heat. Preheat oven to 200°C.

In an oiled casserole dish layer the sauce, eggplant, sauce, eggplant, sauce. Bake for 20 minutes or more until bubbly.

Buckwheat Pilaf

2 cups buckwheat	1 tsp herb salt
3¾ cups water·	3 tbs sesame seeds

Bring buckwheat, water and salt to the boil. Boil for 5 minutes, covered. Then turn off heat and cover pot with a thick towel to trap in heat. Let sit undisturbed for 10 minutes or more.

Toast sesame seeds and serve over buckwheat.

Carrot Sticks

carrots

Slice into sticks and serve.

---

76 Eggplant Coconut Cream   *SERVES 4-6*

- *Eggplant in Coconut Cream* •
- *Baked Pumpkin Tahini* •
- *Red Salad* •

Light, nourishing with a rainbow of colours, flavours and textures. The eggplant dish in particular and the whole style of the meal is of Caribbean heritage.

Preparation Plan
- prepare and bake eggplant
- bake pumpkin
- prepare salad, and serve

Eggplant In Coconut Cream

2 medium eggplant	2 cups coconut cream
1 cup finely chopped onions	juice of 1 lemon
one of the folowing protein options:	1 tsp finely chopped garlic
1-2 blocks tofu, crumbled	2 tsp paprika
1-2 sliced boneless chicken breasts	½ tsp mixed herbs
1½ cups fresh, tinned or smoked fish	herb salt

Preheat oven to 200ºC. Thinly slice the eggplant and prepare the other ingredients. Combine milk with lemon juice, garlic and seasonings.

In an oiled casserole dish layer eggplant, onion and protein option, finishing with the eggplant. Pour in milk mixture. Cover tightly with foil and bake for 20 minutes. Remove foil and bake for 10 minutes or more until eggplant is lightly browned.

Baked Pumpkin Tahini

thin pumpkin slices	tahini
honey	mixed spice or ginger

Place slices in one layer in an oiled casserole dish. Drizzle with honey and tahini and sprinkle with mixed spice or ginger. Bake in the oven with eggplant for 20 minutes or more until tender.

Red Salad

tomato segments	celery, angle-cut
thin red pepper slices	olive oil

Toss vegetables and drizzle with olive oil.

77   *Toad in the Hole* SERVES 4

- *Toad in the Hole with Tofu or Sausages* •
  - *Baked Tomatoes* •
- *Brussels Sprouts Sweet and Sesame* •

Toad in the Hole is a favourite British dish — not exactly coq au vin but still a homey classic. Sausages are the traditional main ingredient but breaded lengths of tofu are another option. For better consistency and rising ability it is best to whizz the batter in a blender in advance by at least one hour: first thing in the morning would be fine — taking only 5 minutes of your time — and then it would be all ready for dinner preparation.

Preparation Plan
- prepare batter and chill; prepare tofu, top with batter and bake
- bake tomatoes
- steam vegetables; toss and serve

Toad in the Hole

Batter:
2 eggs
1 cup flour (wheat is best)
1 cup milk (soy, cow, goat, coconut cream)
herb salt
dash cayenne

½kg small pork sausages or 2 blocks tofu,
   sliced lengthwise into 8 "sausages"

Coating:
¼ cup rice flour or other
¼ cup bread or cracker crumbs
1 tsp paprika
1 tsp mixed herbs
1 tsp curry powder
herb salt

2 tbs melted fat, butter or margarine

Whizz all batter ingredients in the blender for one minute. Refrigerate for at least one hour.

Preheat oven to 200ºC. Either fry sausages or combine coating ingredients in a plastic bag, add one tofu "sausage" at a time and shake to coat. Fry tofu over a medium heat until crisp.

Place sausages or tofu in one layer in an oiled baking dish. Drizzle with the melted fat or option. Pour the batter over top and bake for 30 minutes or until the batter has risen and is crisp and brown. Serve at once.

Baked Tomatoes

tomatoes sliced in halves or thirds
soy sauce

cayenne

Place thick slices of tomato in an oiled pan and sprinkle with soy sauce and cayenne. Bake alongside the Toad in the Hole for about 10 minutes until very hot.

Brussels Sprouts Sweet and Sesame

brussels sprouts
cauliflower or parsnips
onion rings

2 tbs tahini or toasted sesame seeds
1 tsp honey

Steam vegetables for 5-10 minutes until tender. Drain and toss with remaining ingredients.

Curry and Custard

• *Baked Curry with Custard Topping — with Lamb or Tofu* •
• *Chinese Cabbage Salad* •

Of South African origin — where such a mixture is called a "bobotie" — this mild and fruity curry is baked with a golden custard on top. Traditionally this is made with ground lamb but I also include a tofu alternative. A crisp tossed salad or coleslaw is an ideal accompaniment.

Preparation Plan
- fry meat or tofu; bring to the boil with veg. and seasonings; top with custard and bake
- prepare salad, and serve

Baked Curry with Custard Topping

3cm slice bread, broken into bits
1 cup milk (soy, cow, goat, coconut cream)

3 tbs cold-pressed oil
600g lean ground lamb or cubed tofu
½ cup finely chopped onions
¼ cup coarsely chopped almonds
1-3 tsp curry powder
⅓ cup lemon juice

1 tbs molasses
¼ tsp sage
¼ tsp thyme
herb salt
2 medium sweet potatoes, cubed
8 brussels sprouts, quartered
1 large tart apple, grated
⅓ cup sultanas or currants
3 eggs

Preheat the oven to 160ºC. Soak the bread in the millk for at least 10 minutes, then strain and squeeze, reserving milk.

Fry the meat or tofu in the oil over a medium heat for several minutes until either no pink remains in the meat or the tofu is browned and crisp. Stir in the onions and nuts and cook for 3 minutes until the onions are softened. Add the curry powder and cook for 2 minutes. Stir in lemon juice, molasses, herb salt and vegetables and bring to the boil.

Remove from heat and stir in the apple, sultanas, one egg and the squeezed bread until well combined. Pour into a greased, deep 3-litre casserole dish.

Beat the 2 eggs with the reserved milk for one minute or until frothy. Pour over the curry and bake for 20-30 minutes until the custard is a light golden brown.

Chinese Cabbage Salad

2 cups grated or well-chopped
   Chinese cabbage
1 cup grated carrot

½ cup cucumber in small cubes
3 tbs Homemade Mayonnaise
3 tbs relish

Toss the vegetables together, then blend the mayonnaise and relish, and thoroughly combine with the vegetables until well moistened. Keep covered and chill until serving time.

79 *Topfenknödel* SERVES 4-6

- *Cheese or Tofu Dumplings* •
- *Vegetables Paprikash* •
- *Sour Courgette Salad* •

Topfenknödel is the Austrian name for cottage cheese dumplings. There they are often prepared as a sweet and served with jam or stewed fruit.

Preparation Plan
- boil and grill dumplings
- prepare vegetables
- prepare salad, and serve

Cheese or Tofu Dumplings

500g cottage cheese or mashed tofu	1 tsp herb salt
8 tbs melted butter or margarine	1 tsp dill seed
3 tbs chopped chives	3 cups rice flour or other
1 tbs prepared mustard	¾ cup bread or cracker crumbs

Combine cottage cheese, 4 tablespoons of the melted butter, and the seasonings. Beat in the flour a few tablespoons at a time until the mixture becomes a medium firm dough.

In a large saucepan bring to the boil about 2 litres water. Form dough into balls about 5cm in diameter and drop them into the boiling water. Reduce the heat to low and simmer the dumplings, uncovered, for about 15 minutes, turning them occasionally with a slotted spoon. Drain them on a kitchen towel or 2 layers of paper towels.

Place the dumplings in a shallow heatproof dish or gratin pan and toss with 2 tablespoons of the butter. Sprinkle with breadcrumbs and drizzle with remaining butter. Grill carefully until crisp.

Vegetables Paprikash

cabbage, chopped	3 tbs cold-pressed oil
parsnip, sliced	2 tsp coriander
green beans, sliced	1 tsp paprika

Steam vegetables until just tender. Toss with remaining ingredients and serve.

Sour Courgette Salad

3-4 courgettes, cubed	2 tbs apple cider vinegar
1 large gherkin, diced	1 tbs prepared mustard

Toss courgettes with remaining ingredients. Cover and chill until serving time.

• Potato Dumplings •
• Avocado Slices •
• Winter Vegetable Medley •

Another easy, filling dish of Teutonic origins. Bacon, cheese, smoked fish or other savoury additions can be made to the dumpling batter. The avocado is an appropriately rich and creamy accompaniment.

Preparation Plan
- mash potatoes; prepare dough; simmer
- steam vegetables
- slice avocado, and serve

Potato Dumplings

4-5 medium potatoes	1 tsp mixed herbs
¼ cup butter or margarine	herb salt
1 cup bread or cracker crumbs	½ tsp nutmeg
½ cup pumpkin kernels	2 eggs
3 tbs sesame seeds	
1 cup rice flour	extra flour
1 tsp curry powder	1 tsp seasalt

Steam potatoes and mash to make 3½ cups.

Meanwhile over a medium heat melt the butter and toast the breadcrumbs, kernels and seeds until light brown and crisp. Set aside.

Beat flour and seasonings and half the toasted mixture into the potatoes. Lightly beat the eggs, then beat into potato mixture.

Bring 3 litres water and one teaspoon salt to a rolling boil. Lightly flour hands and shape each dumpling using about 3 tablespoons of dough at a time. Drop all the dumplings into the boiling water and stir gently once or twice to prevent them from sticking. Simmer over a medium heat for 12-15 minutes or until they rise to the surface. Cook for one minute longer, then remove dumplings with a slotted spoon and place on a heated platter.

Sprinkle with the remaining toasted mixture and serve at once.

Winter Vegetable Medley

cauliflower segments	spring onions, chopped
carrots in sticks	2 tbs cold-pressed oil
brussels sprouts, halved	juice of 1 small lemon
sliced mushrooms	1 tsp curry powder

Steam all vegetables — except spring onions — until tender. Toss with remaining ingredients and serve.

Avocado Slices

1-2 ripe avocados	paprika

Peel and slice the avocados, and serve sprinkled with paprika.

81 *Potato Pat-a-Cake*

- *Potato or Kumara (Sweet Potato) Patties — Mashed or Hashed!* •
  - *Mixed Vegetable Hot Pot* •
  - *Cucumber with Mint Mayonnaise or Yoghurt* •

About 12 different menus can be spawned from this one. Patties are formed in either of two ways: mashed potato or kumara is flavoured, formed into thin patties and grilled, or a la hashed browns — grated potato or kumara is flavoured, spooned into shape, and fried or baked. Other grated vegetables can be likewise experimented with: courgette, carrot, pumpkin, marrow.

Preparation Plan
- prepare choice of patties
- steam and toss vegetables
- prepare dressing and cucumber, and serve

Potato or Kumara Patties

3-4 potatoes or equivalent kumara
  to make 3 cups mashed or grated
3 eggs for mashed mixture or
  4 eggs for hashed mixture
¼ cup food yeast (optional)
¼ cup rice flour or other

½ cup pumpkin kernels
4 spring onions, chopped
1 tsp curry powder
½ tsp bouquet garni
½ tsp sage
herb salt to taste

If using the mashed method, scrub, cube and steam potatoes until soft — for about 5 minutes. Mash. Combine mashed or grated vegetable with remaining ingredients.

Mashed method: form into thin patties, drizzle with oil (optional) and grill until crisp on both sides.

Hashed method: dollop thin rounds of mixture on an oiled baking pan and bake at 220ºC for 20 minutes turning once or dollop in frypan and fry in batches.

Mixed Vegetable Hot Pot

seasonal mixed vegetables such as:
  carrot sticks; brussels sprouts, halved;
  angle-cut celery; whole baby mushrooms

1½ tbs natural soy sauce
1 tbs cold-pressed oil
1 tbs molasses

Steam vegetable medley for 5-10 minutes until crisply tender. Toss with the remaining ingredients.

Cucumber with Mint Mayonnaise or Yoghurt

cucumber
fresh mint

Homemade Mayonnaise or yoghurt

Slice cucumber. Mix ample fresh mint with mayonnaise or yoghurt. Serve alongside the cucumber.

- *Reuben Rolls* -
- *Mustard Sauce* -
- *Baby Carrots with Ginger Glaze* -

In America a Reuben sandwich is one with mustard, sauerkraut, Swiss cheese and corned beef (similar to silverside). Here rice, sauerkraut and other ingredients are mixed into scrumptious croquettes and served with a tangy mustard sauce.

Preparation Plan
- pre-cook rice; prepare croquettes
- prepare carrots
- prepare sauce, and serve

Reuben Rolls

2 cups brown rice
3½ cups water or Stock
herb salt

2 eggs
1 tsp mixed herbs
½ tsp powdered ginger
¼ tsp nutmeg

450g sauerkraut
¾ cup toasted pumpkin kernels or chopped
   smoked fish or corned beef or silverside
1 large onion
1 cup finely chopped spinach or silverbeet
¾ cup pineapple pieces

optional Crispy Coating:
rice flour or other
1 egg
2 tbs milk
1¼ cups fine bread or cracker crumbs

Bring rice, salt and water to the boil, covered. Boil for 10 minutes undisturbed. Turn off heat and cover top and sides of pan with a thick towel to steam-cook. Do not disturb for 30 minutes or longer. The rice may then sit all day if necessary.

Drain and squeeze sauerkraut to rid it of excess liquid. Chop very fine along with onion, fish or meat (if using pumpkin kernels leave them whole). Combine with remaining ingredients. Using about ¼ cup mixture for each roll, form into croquettes.

If you have extra time make the Crispy Coating: roll each croquette in flour, then dip in mixture of beaten egg and milk, then again in flour or in crumbs.

Fry or bake in well-oiled pan at 230ºC for 15-20 minutes until crisp, turning once.

Baby Carrots with Ginger Glaze

8-12 small carrots
1 tbs cold-pressed oil

1 tbs grated, peeled ginger root
herb salt

Steam carrots whole for 5-10 minutes, until just tender. Toss with remaining ingredients.

Mustard Sauce

½ cup Homemade Mayonnaise
½ cup cream or coconut cream

¼ cup or more prepared mustard
2 tbs lemon juice

Combine all ingredients. Taste for desired piquancy, adding more mustard if necessary. Serve at room temperature.

- *Spinach Fritters with Fish or Tofu* •
  - *Peanut Sauce* •
- *Asian Winter Salad* •

More simple patties and these ones are made without eggs. The Peanut Sauce is a popular and flavourful accompaniment and any left-over can be served as a delicious salad dressing the next day. The Asian dressing is a good one for marinating cucumber or other vegetables in, to accompany Chinese-style foods.

Preparation Plan
- prepare fritters and bake or fry
- prepare sauce
- prepare salad, and serve

Spinach Fritters

1½ cups chopped or flaked raw or
   tinned fish or
   1½ cups cubed tofu
1½ cups well-chopped spinach
1 cup grated carrot

¾ cup bread or cracker crumbs
¾ cup yoghurt or coconut cream
2 tbs cold-pressed oil
2 tsp curry powder
herb salt

Combine all the ingredients. Add more breadcrumbs to thicken or more yoghurt or cream to moisten, if necessary.

Dollop mixture into a frypan and fry, or into a well-oiled baking pan and bake at 200°C for 20 minutes or longer, turning once, until crisp.

Peanut Sauce

3 cups Vegetable Stock
5 tbs rice flour or other
¼ cup peanut butter
3 tbs natural soy sauce

3cm peeled ginger root
1-4 cloves garlic
2 tsp coriander
1 tsp garam masala

Whizz all the ingredients in a blender. Pour into a saucepan and bring to the boil. Simmer for 10 minutes or longer.

Asian Winter Salad

Dressing:
3 tbs apple cider vinegar
1 tbs natural soy sauce
1 tbs honey
1 tsp Chinese 5-spice powder
dash cayenne

broccoli
cauliflower
mung bean sprouts
sliced mushrooms

Combine the dressing ingredients in a salad bowl.

Slice broccoli and cauliflower into small segments and add with remaining vegetables to the dressing, and toss. Serve or cover, chill and allow to marinate before serving.

- *Potato Sausages* •
- *Mushroom Gravy* •
- *Four Vegetable Salad* •

The "sausages" are a fun concoction children should approve of. If you wish to include meat, some lean ground beef can be added to the potato mixture. Just be sure to give them longer cooking time.

Preparation Plan
- steam and mash potatoes; flavour and form into "sausages"; grill
- prepare gravy
- prepare salad, and serve

Potato Sausages

4 large potatoes
¾ cup peanuts or sunflower seed kernels
3 eggs
1 small onion, finely chopped
1 tsp finely chopped garlic
¼ cup chopped parsley
1 tsp mixed herbs
¼ tsp allspice
¼ tsp sage

herb salt

Coating:
½ cup rice flour
½ tsp turmeric
herb salt

oil for grilling

Chop potatoes into small pieces and steam for about 5 minutes until tender; mash.

Meanwhile toast nuts or seeds and grind. Beat eggs into potato mixture. Stir in remaining ingredients. Cool as much as possible before shaping.

Combine the coating ingredients in a shallow bowl. Form potato mixture into sausage shapes and roll in coating to cover. Drizzle with oil and grill on both sides until crisp.

Mushroom Gravy

2½ cups Vegetable Stock
5 tbs rice flour or other
3 tbs miso or marmite
1 tbs peanut butter

1 tsp tarragon
1 tsp oreganum
½ tsp mild curry powder
2 bay leaves

Bring all the ingredients to the boil, then simmer for 10 minutes or more until thick and flavourful. Taste for seasoning.

Four Vegetable Salad

Dressing:
3 tbs cold-pressed oil
1 tbs honey
1 tbs prepared mustard
juice of 1 small lemon

celery, sliced
tomatoes, sliced
courgettes, sliced
fresh peas

Combine the dressing ingredients in a salad bowl.

Toss with the vegetables. Cover and chill until serving time.

85   *Pineapple Rounds*   *SERVES 4*

• *Pineapple Rounds with Peanut Topping* •
• *Mashed Sweet Potato* •
• *Spiced Cauliflower Salad* •

The Pineapple Rounds can be served hot or cold or in a bite-sized portion as an hors d'oeuvre.

Preparation Plan
- slice pineapple and top
- steam and mash sweet potatoes
- prepare salad; grill pineapple, and serve

Pineapple Rounds with Peanut Topping

1 small fresh pineapple

½ cup peanuts
3 tbs peanut butter
2 tbs soy sauce
2 tsp coriander
1 tsp finely chopped ginger root

1 tsp finely chopped garlic
1 tsp honey
½ cup water

few tbs bread or cracker crumbs or mashed tofu or chopped fresh or cooked fish or chopped cooked meat, to thicken

Slice pineapple into thick 10mm slices, allowing about 2 per person.

Toast peanuts until lightly browned. Stir in remaining ingredients (except bread or option) and bring to the boil. Remove from heat and stir in bread or option. Place a mound of topping at the centre of each round. Five minutes before serving, place under the grill to brown.

Mashed Sweet Potato

4 large sweet potato or kumara

Coarsely chop the sweet potato and steam until tender. Mash while incorporating some of the steaming liquid until the mixture is of desired consistency.

Spiced Cauliflower Salad

cauliflower segments
shredded cabbage
2 chopped spring onions
3 tbs cold-pressed oil

1 tsp cumin powder
1 tsp honey
herb salt

Toss all the ingredients until well combined.

- *Savoury Sesame Grill with Fish or Tofu or Chicken* •
- *Cucumber Sauce* •
- *Whole Baby Vegetables with Salad Garnish* •

A succulent and colourful quickie. Fish fillets or steaks, large slices of tofu, or thin slices of chicken breast are coated and grilled. As an accompaniment there is a creamy, whizz-in-the-blender, room temperature cucumber sauce.

Preparation Plan
- prepare sauce
- ready vegetables, then steam while preparing protein option
- coat and grill protein option

Cucumber Sauce

1 medium telegraph cucumber	2 tbs fresh chopped mint or
1 block tofu or 1 cup cottage cheese	1 tsp dried mint
1 cup Homemade Mayonnaise or	2 tbs fresh chopped dill or 1 tsp dill seed
1 cup coconut cream	dash cayenne
2 tbs apple cider vinegar	herb salt

Peel and cube half the cucumber; reserve.

Chop remaining cucumber and place in a blender with remaining ingredients. Whizz until smooth and thick. Taste for seasoning. Pour into a bowl or sauceboat and stir in reserved cucumber. Cover until serving time. Chill if preferred.

Whole Baby Vegetables with Salad Garnish

small carrots	2 tbs cold-pressed oil
mushrooms	1 tbs coriander
small courgettes	bean sprouts

Ready the vegetables in the pot and cook for about 15 minutes before serving time.

Steam vegetables until tender, for about 10 minutes. Drain and toss with oil and coriander. Serve — perhaps on a platter alongside the fish or option — and surround with bean sprouts.

Savoury Sesame Grill

one of the following protein options:	3 tbs sesame seeds
fish fillets or steaks	1 tsp curry powder
2 blocks tofu in horizontal slices	½ tsp turmeric
filleted chicken breasts, sliced	herb salt
¼ cup rice flour or other	cold-pressed oil

Combine coating ingredients in a plastic bag. A few pieces at a time, add a choice of protein option and shake to completely cover. Place on grill plate and drizzle with oil. Grill for 5-10 minutes on each side until crisp and golden; serve.

- *Stuffed Sesame Tomatoes and Courgettes* •
  - *Pasta or Potatoes* •
- *Parmesan Spinach Salad* •

In countries all round the Mediterranean vegetables are filled and baked, grilled or stewed with succulent success. Take a rice or potato or nut and seed filling from one recipe and fill your choice of vegetable, heat and serve. Here both courgettes and tomatoes are used with a super-quick tofu filling. Cottage cheese could be used instead, in which case omit the soy sauce.

Preparation Plan
- prepare filling; grill stuffed vegetables
- cook pasta or potatoes
- prepare salad, and serve

Sesame Stuffed Tomatoes and Courgettes

2 cups mashed tofu	chopped parsley
½ cup toasted pinenuts or peanuts	4-8 courgettes
¼ cup peanut butter or tahini	4-8 tomatoes (quantity depends
2 tbs olive oil	on size of vegetable)
2 tbs soy sauce	basil
3 spring onions, chopped	olive oil

Slice tomatoes and courgettes in half horizontally. Scoop out inner flesh leaving a secure shell.

Combine remaining ingredients and pack into vegetable shells. Sprinkle with basil and drizzle with olive oil. Grill not too close to the heat so there is time (about 10 minutes) to cook through.

Pasta or Potatoes

pasta or 4-6 large potatoes	1 tsp basil
2 tbs olive oil	1 tsp cumin powder
2 tbs lemon juice	herb salt

Cook pasta to packet instructions or slice potatoes into quarters or sixths and steam until just cooked. Toss either choice with remaining ingredients and serve.

Parmesan Spinach Salad

spinach leaves, broken	olive oil
red pepper, sliced	parmesan cheese
bean sprouts	

Arrange vegetables on a large platter. Drizzle with olive oil and sprinkle with parmesan.

- *Mixed Grill — Vegetarian or Seafood or Meat* •
- *Texas Barbecue Sauce* •
- *Coleslaw* •

This is an especially quick meal, light but rich with spunky flavour. Heartier appetites might prefer the addition of boiled rice or a steamed starchy vegetable. Any left-over sauce (unlikely I admit) is great cold as a relish.

Preparation Plan
- prepare sauce
- prepare coleslaw
- prepare choice of mixed grill, and serve

Texas Barbecue Sauce

5-6 medium tomatoes, chopped	3 tbs brown sugar
1 green pepper, sliced	2½ tbs natural soy sauce
1 large onion, sliced	2 tbs prepared mustard
lots of garlic!	dash cayenne
oil for frying	2-3 tsp rice flour or other
3 tbs apple cider vinegar	

Fry vegetables over a brisk heat until tender. Add remaining ingredients and bring to the boil. Simmer briskly for 10 minutes or more. Sprinkle in rice flour as you stir, to thicken sauce slightly.

Coleslaw

grated cabbage	toasted sesame seeds
grated carrot	Homemade Mayonnaise or yoghurt
mung or lentil or wheat beansprouts	

Combine all ingredients. Cover and chill until serving time.

Mixed Grill

Choose one of the three options, drizzle any of the non-fatty foods with olive oil, and grill on both sides until crisp and tender. Watch carefully.

VEGETARIAN	SEAFOOD	MEAT
2 large eggplant, unpeeled, in 10mm slices	vegetables as for Vegetarian option	vegetables as for Vegetarian option
courgettes, halved lengthwise	one or more of the following:	one or more of the following:
10mm slices tempeh or tofu	fish fillets	chicken breast
	fish roe	chicken livers
	squid rings	bacon
	mussels	ham
		sausage
		salami

- *Brazilian Rice* -
- *Cheese Topping* -
- *Grilled Eggplant and Courgette Slices* -

This takes an especially brief preparation time and is another Latin American specialty of a similar nature to Cuban Rice. The rice is cooked with lots of tomato and onion and will be of a wetter risotto-style when cooked. The cheese used for the topping can be a sheep or goats' milk feta for those on milk-restricted diets. Or use grilled or fried cubes of tofu sprinkled with soy sauce.

Preparation Plan
- prepare rice
- grill vegetables
- ready cheese and sprinkle over rice, and serve

Brazilian Rice

4 tbs olive oil
2 large onions, thinly sliced
2 cups brown rice
3½ cups water or Vegetable Stock

2 large tomatoes, coarsely chopped
1-3 cloves garlic, chopped
8 olives, whole or chopped
herb salt

Cook onion in oil until tender but not brown. Add rice and cook over a medium heat for 2-3 minutes. Add remaining ingredients and bring to the boil. Cover and let boil for 10 minutes, undisturbed. Turn off heat, cover top and sides of pan with a thick towel and leave undisturbed for 20 minutes or longer.

Cheese Topping
ample grated cheese or crumbled feta

Serve rice on a large heated platter and cover with cheese to slightly melt before serving. Or use tofu option as outlined above.

Grilled Eggplant and Courgette Slices

1-2 medium eggplant
4-8 courgettes
olive oil

Coating:
4 tbs rice flour or other
1 tsp oreganum
1 tsp curry powder
½ tsp turmeric
herb salt

Slice courgettes in half lengthwise. Slice eggplant at its short end into 10mm slices.

Place coating ingredients in a plastic bag and add 2 or 3 eggplant slices at a time. Shake to coat evenly.

Place slices under grill with courgettes (if you have to do this in two batches do the eggplant first as it takes longest to cook; keep warm in a low oven while doing courgettes). Drizzle with olive oil and grill for about 5 minutes on each side until eggplant is crisp and well cooked; be careful not to overcook courgettes. Keep warm until serving time.

- *Rumaki with Chicken Livers or Fish or Tofu*
  - *Striped Potatoes*
    - *Corn Salad*

Rumaki is a Hawaiian kebab dish, traditionally with chicken livers, water chestnuts and bacon. Here the threaded skewers are soaked in a flavourful broth before grilling (commonly they are deep fried). The broth can then be served in small bowls beside each plate as a dipping sauce.

Preparation Plan
- prepare sauce and skewers
- prepare potatoes
- prepare salad; grill skewers, and serve

Rumaki

Broth:
½ cup soy sauce
½ cup brown sugar
½ cup water
8cm length ginger root,
    peeled and crushed
5cm stick cinnamon
1 large clove garlic, crushed

8 star anise
2 bay leaves

Skewers:
½ kg chicken livers or
    2 blocks tofu, cubed or
    ½ kg fish, cubed
12 tinned water chestnuts, halved

In a saucepan (wide enough to hold a skewer laid flat) bring all broth ingredients to the boil and simmer for 10 minutes.

Meanwhile thread on skewer selection.

About 15 minutes before serving, immerse skewers in the broth and simmer gently for 3 minutes. With a slotted spoon remove skewers to the grill and grill for about 3 minutes on each side until crisp.

Strain broth into small bowls and place beside each dinner plate.

Striped Potatoes

4 medium potatoes, sliced into eighths
1 small red pepper, thinly sliced
1 small green pepper, thinly sliced
3 tbs cold-pressed oil

2 tsp basil
1 tsp paprika
herb salt

Steam potatoes and peppers (the stripes) until just tender. Drain and toss with the remaining ingredients.

Corn Salad

1 cup corn
sliced mushrooms
few chopped silverbeet leaves

2 tbs chopped chives
1 gherkin, diced

Combine all ingredients and serve.

91 *Peppercorn Pinwheels* SERVES 3-4

• *Port and Peppercorn Pinwheels and Sauce*
with Chicken or Veal or Fish or Squid or Eggplant and Cheese •
• *Paprika Vegetable Medley* •
• *Bean Sprouts Garnish* •

With its more exotic ingredients this is ideal for entertaining. Or omit the peppercorns for less adventurous diners and try the vegetarian eggplant version for an economical family meal.

Preparation Plan
- cook chicken or option
- steam and toss vegetables
- arrange sprouts, and serve

Port and Peppercorn Chicken or Veal Pinwheels

2 chicken breasts, skinned and boned or 2-4 veal scallopine
2-4 thin slices smoked ham or ⅓ cup crumbled feta cheese (cow, goat or sheep)
⅓ cup chopped mushrooms
½ tsp green peppercorns, crushed
few tsp butter or oil
½ cup white wine
½ cup chicken or Vegetable Stock

1 tbs lemon juice
4 black peppercorns
2 tbs butter or oil

Sauce:
2 tbs rice flour or other
2 tbs redcurrant or other tart jelly
2 tbs Port
1 tsp green peppercorns, crushed

Preheat oven to 190°C.

Lay each chicken or veal slice flat and cover with one spinach leaf, ham or cheese, mushrooms and half teaspoon green peppercorns. Roll up snugly and secure with a metal skewer. Fry in butter or oil until golden. Place in a greased ovenproof dish with wine, stock, lemon juice, black peppercorns and butter or oil. Cover with foil and bake for 20 minutes until tender.

Remove chicken rolls to a warm place. Strain off pan juices into a small saucepan, then stir in flour, jelly and green peppercorns. Bring to the boil; simmer for 5 minutes. Stir in Port and salt to taste.

Carve the rolls into 15mm slices and serve accompanied with the sauce.

or Fish or Squid Pinwheels

Prepare as above except use fish fillets or squid tubes (gut, clean and slice tubes at one long end to give a flat surface). Omit frying stage. Bake for 15 minutes or until tender.

or **Vegetarian Eggplant Pinwheels**

1-2 large eggplant
few extra spinach leaves

extra feta cheese

Slice eggplant into 10mm slices. Lightly brush with oil on both sides and grill for 3-5 minutes on each side until limp and grey.

Prepare as above omitting the frying stage. Bake for 15-20 minutes and continue as above. Omit salt; serve whole or thickly sliced.

Paprika Vegetable Medley

whole baby potatoes
large broccoli segments
onion rings

few tsp cold-pressed oil
1 tsp paprika
herb salt or food yeast

Steam potatoes and onion rings for about 10 minutes until almost cooked. Add broccoli to the pot and steam for 3-5 minutes until crisply tender. Remove from heat, remove steamer, and reserve stock for other use. Add oil and seasonings, and toss.

Bean Sprouts Garnish

Use bean sprouts to surround the pinwheel slices on the serving plate.

• *Rice Wrappers with choice of fillings* •
• *Coconut Sauce* •
• *Cauliflower Cucumber Salad* •

For wonton-lovers (take that any way you like). These noodle-wrappers are made from rice flour and sold in round or triangular shapes in Asian specialty stores. The wrappers need only be dipped in tap water to be soft and ready for filling, rolling, then steaming or baking.

Preparation Plan
- prepare filling; dip, fill and bake wrappers
- prepare sauce
- prepare salad, and serve

Rice Wrappers and Fillings

Filling:
cold-pressed oil
1½ cups finely chopped cabbage
1 medium onion, chopped
2-4 cloves garlic, chopped
¼ cup chopped mushrooms
2 tsp cumin powder
2 tbs natural soy sauce

Protein options:
  ½ cup sunflower seed kernels

½ cup peanuts
¾ cup diced raw fish
¾ cup chopped chicken livers
¾ cup finely sliced beef or
  pork steak or chicken breast
¾ cup chopped left-over cooked meat
4 egg omelette, chopped

Rice wrappers:
16-20 round or triangular
rice-noodle wrappers

Stir-fry all ingredients (except soy sauce) — including one protein option — until vegetables are tender. Stir in soy sauce. Remove from heat to cool slightly for easier handling. Preheat oven to 200ºC.

Dip one wrapper briefly in a bowl of water. Fill, roll and place seam-side down on an oiled baking dish. Brush lightly with oil and bake for 10-15 minutes or more until crisp.

Coconut Sauce

1¼ cups coconut cream
¾ cup Vegetable Stock
1 small onion, diced
3cm peeled ginger root, diced
3 tbs coconut
2-3 tbs rice flour or other

2 tbs peanut butter
1 tbs honey
1 tbs lemon juice
1 tsp coriander
¼ tsp nutmeg
herb salt

Bring ingredients to the boil and simmer for 10 minutes or more. Sprinkle and whisk in more rice flour for increased thickening if necessary.

Cauliflower Cucumber Salad

cucumber
cauliflower
2 tbs apple cider vinegar

1 tbs natural soy sauce
1 tbs honey
chilli powder to taste

Peel and slice cucumber. Chop cauliflower into small pieces. Toss with remaining ingredients. If there is time, cover and allow to marinate for greater flavour.

93 *Polish Family Dinner* *SERVES 4*

- *Cabbage Rolls with Sunflower Seed Kernels or Sausage* •
- *Vinegared Cucumber and Onion Slices* •

Many nations serve cabbage rolls as a local specialty. This recipe is more a collage of their varying ingredients than strictly Polish. The rice for the filling is cooked the night before or in the morning as a time-saving device. This only requires your presence for 10 minutes as the rice boils. The heat is then turned off and the rice steam-cooks under a thick towel encasing the saucepan. It is a practical and time-saving method worth remembering.

Preparation Plan
- cook rice in advance; prepare cabbage rolls
- marinate salad vegetables, and serve

Cabbage Rolls

2½ cups brown rice
4½ cups water
herb salt

1 whole cabbage

oil or butter
¾ cup sunflower seed kernels or
   spicy sausage
1 large onion

3 sticks celery
1 cup peas or corn
2 tsp mild curry powder
1 tsp mixed herbs
herb salt
1 cup pineapple pieces

3-4 large tomatoes
1 cup sour cream, yoghurt, or coconut cream
paprika

Bring rice, herb salt and water to the boil, covered for 10 minutes. Without lifting the lid, turn off heat and wrap a towel over the top and sides of the pot. Leave undisturbed for 30 minutes or longer.

Slice off base of cabbage and slice and pull off leaves. Steam for 3-5 minutes, just until soft enough to bend. Cut away any hard base which won't bend.

Over a low heat fry sunflower seed kernels, onion, celery and peas or corn until vegetables are tender and seeds crisp. Stir in curry powder, mixed herbs and rice. Cook to reheat rice. Stir in pineapple and taste for seasoning. Preheat oven to 220°C.

Place some of the filling — 3 or 4 tablespoons — on each cabbage leaf. Roll and place in one layer seam-side down on an oiled baking dish (suitable for serving). Surround with any left-over rice mixture.

Cover with slices of tomato, then drizzle with sour cream or option. Sprinkle with paprika. Bake for 10 minutes or more until hot and bubbly.

Vinegared Cucumber and Onion Slices

cucumber slices
red onion rings (optional)
3 tbs apple cider vinegar

1 tbs fresh dill or 1 tsp dill seed
herb salt
freshly ground pepper

Combine all the ingredients. Cover and let sit for 10 minutes or longer.

Oriental Roll-ups

- *Oriental Roll-ups — Vegetarian or Fish or Meat* •
- *Tamarillo Sauce* •
- *Vegetables Golden Pagoda* •

Here a base of either eggplant, cabbage or fish fillets is topped with a spunky carrot filling (with protein options), rolled up and briefly baked. For heartier diners, egg noodles or rice may also be served.

Preparation Plan
- prepare choice of base, then filling with choice of protein option
- prepare sauce
- prepare vegetables, and serve

Oriental Roll-ups

Eggplant Base:
2-3 large eggplant

Cabbage Base:
1 small whole cabbage

Fish Base:
1-2 fish fillets per person

Carrot Filling:
1½ cups grated carrot
3 spring onions, chopped

½ cup drained pineapple pieces
1 tsp powdered ginger
1 tsp Chinese 5-spice powder

Protein options:
½ cup toasted nuts or seeds
1 cup cubed tofu or tempeh
4-egg omelette, sliced
tinned or raw cubed fish
left-over cooked meat

mung bean sprouts

Choose one of the three bases. Either: Take 10mm slices from long end of eggplants. Brush lightly with oil and grill briefly on both sides until dark and limp.
Or: Cut off cabbage base. Slice and pull off whole leaves. Steam for 3-5 minutes until supple.
Or: Wash fish fillets and pat dry. Preheat oven to 190ºC.

Combine all the ingredients (except sprouts) plus one protein option. Place some of the filling on a choice of base. Roll up and place seam-side down on an oiled baking dish (suitable for serving). Bake for 15-20 minutes until hot and tender. Garnish each roll with a drizzle of sauce and some long mung bean sprouts.

Tamarillo Sauce

1 cup pineapple juice
1 cup Vegetable Stock
3 tamarillos, peeled and chopped
4 tbs rice flour or 3 tbs arrowroot

1 tbs molasses
1 tbs brown sugar
2 tbs natural soy sauce
2 tsp coriander

Bring all the ingredients to the boil, then simmer for 10 minutes or longer. Serve in a sauceboat.

Vegetables Golden Pagoda

kumara
cauliflower
baby yellow scallopini-squash
asparagus, green beans or peapods

1 tbs cold-pressed oil
1 tsp coriander
½ tsp turmeric

Slice kumara into rounds and keep remaining vegetables in large pieces. Steam for 5-10 minutes until tender. Toss with oil and spices.

95 *Pumpkin Wedges*

- *Pumpkin Wedges* •
- *Sunflower Topping* •
- *German Green Bean Salad* •

An economical winter-time menu. The bright colour of the pumpkin is a designer's delight. Remember this type of seed — or nut — topping for stuffing courgettes, mushrooms (as an appetiser), marrow, onion, eggplant, tomato and peppers.

Preparation Plan
- prepare pumpkin
- prepare topping, mound on pumpkin and bake
- prepare salad, and serve

Pumpkin Wedges

pumpkin	cinnamon
cold-pressed oil	

Slice pumpkin into large attractive slices, about 2 per person. Place in one layer in a large, oiled baking dish. Lightly brush with oil and sprinkle with cinnamon. Preheat oven to 200°C.

Prepare topping and place in a ball — like an ice-cream scoop — on the pumpkin, or nestled in its curve where the seeds were. Bake for 20-30 minutes until pumpkin is tender and topping crisp.

Sunflower Topping

1 cup sunflower seed kernels	½ cup yoghurt (cow, goat) or
2 eggs	Savoury Tofu Whip
1 small onion, diced	2 tbs natural soy sauce
¾ cup bread or cracker crumbs	2 tsp cumin powder
3 tbs cold-pressed oil	½ tsp bouquet garni

Toast seeds. Coarsely grind in a blender. In a bowl combine seeds with the remaining ingredients.

German Green Bean Salad

green beans	2 tbs lemon juice
mung bean sprouts	1 tsp grated lemon peel
radishes, sliced	1 tsp paprika
mushrooms, sliced	1 tsp honey
	1 tsp prepared mustard
Dressing:	herb salt
3 tbs cold-pressed oil	

Steam beans until just tender. Combine the dressing ingredients in a salad bowl and toss with beans. Stir in the remaining vegetables. Cover and chill until serving time, stirring occasionally.

- *Baked or Roast Potatoes with Topping: Mediterranean Medley or Fish or Tofu or Tempeh or Avocado or Egg or Nut and Seed* •
- *Corn on the Cob or Asparagus or Broccoli* •
- *Beetroot Salad* •

Economical, sustaining, yet light and nourishing, this is one of our favourite stand-bys. And with so many toppings to choose from you can serve it often without danger of monotony.

Preparation Plan
- bake potatoes
- prepare choice of topping
- steam choice of vegetable
- prepare salad, and serve

Potatoes

4-8 large potatoes

Preheat oven to 200°C. Scrub potatoes and cut in half for quicker cooking. Either place cut side up in the oven and bake for 35-40 minutes, or put a few teaspoons of oil in an electric frypan and cook them at 180°C for 30 minutes.

Toppings

The principle here is to choose one of the creamy bases and combine it with one of the protein options.

CREAMY BASES:

- Savoury Tofu Whip
  (recipe follows)
- Homemade Mayonnaise
  (recipe follows)
- ricotta or cottage cheese
- yoghurt or sour cream
- half yoghurt,
  half cream cheese, mixed

PROTEIN OPTIONS:

- mashed or cubed avocado
- cubed grilled tempeh or tofu
- fresh cooked fish, chopped
- sardines or salmon or tuna
- hard-boiled eggs
- one or more types toasted nuts and/or seeds
- crumbled blue vein or feta
- Mediterranean Medley: grill tomato, green pepper and eggplant slices, chop, and mix with garlic' and few tablespoons tahini or peanut butter or grated cheese

Savoury Tofu Whip

1 block tofu
3 tbs cold-pressed oil
2 tbs apple cider vinegar
2-3 tsp honey

1-2 tsp cumin powder
½ tsp each: paprika
   mustard powder
herb salt (to taste)

Whizz all ingredients in a blender until creamy.

This is also excellent as a dip or salad dressing. The flavour and texture improve if it is allowed to sit covered and chilled for an hour or overnight.

Homemade Mayonnaise

1 large egg or ¼ cup cold soymilk
2 tbs apple cider vinegar
1-2 tsp honey
½ tsp paprika
½ tsp mustard powder
herb salt to taste
1-1½ cups cold-pressed oil

Place all the ingredients (except oil) in a blender and whizz to combine. Then with speed on slow, slowly dribble in oil until of desired consistency — the more oil the thicker it will be. It will also thicken more with chilling.

There are many flavour variations such as the addition of spices, fresh or dried herbs, grated lemon peel, spring onion, toasted sesame seeds, etc.

Steamed Vegetable

corn on the cob or asparagus or broccoli

Steam for 5 minutes (for broccoli) to 15 minutes (for corn).

Beetroot Salad

There are already lots of flavours and textures to the meal and the creamy topping bypasses the need for a dressing, so the salad can simply be a plate of grated beetroot. Garnish with mint leaves or lemon wedges.

- *Tomatoes Provencale* •
- *Kumara (Sweet Potato) Salad* •
- *Sardine or Peanut Dressing* •

Pretend that you're in southern France with this one — or southern Waikato thanks to the inclusion of the kumara. This is a wonderful summertime menu when tomatoes are abundant and appetites light — beware of the garlicky filling.

Preparation Plan
- halve, fill and bake tomatoes
- prepare salad
- prepare dressing, and serve

Tomatoes Provencale

6 large firm ripe tomatoes
1¼ cups dry bread or
   cracker crumbs
½ cup finely chopped parsley

2 tsp basil
1 large clove garlic, finely chopped
about ⅓ cup olive oil
herb salt

Slice tomatoes in half crosswise and scoop out flesh. Sprinkle interiors with salt. Preheat oven to 190ºC.

Combine breadcrumbs, herbs, garlic and salt. Add enough olive oil to moisten but leave mixture crumbly.

Fill each tomato half. Arrange in a shallow, oiled baking dish; do not crowd. Drizzle with olive oil. Bake for 20 minutes until tomatoes are tender but not limp. These can be served hot or cold.

Kumara (Sweet Potato) Salad

kumara, cubed
broccoli in small segments

fresh peas or cooked corn
sliced mushrooms

Steam kumara for about 5 minutes until soft. Toss with the remaining ingredients.

Sardine or Peanut Dressing

2 tins sardines, drained or
   ¼ cup peanut butter

1 cup Homemade Mayonnaise
chopped chives or spring onions

Coarsely chop sardines and add them (or option) to the remaining ingredients.

- *Stuffed Onions* •
- *Spicy Pumpkin* •
- *Tomato and Cabbage Salad* •

Good winter fare. Of course a meat, cheese, nut or seed filling could be used in place of the fish, and instead of onions, tomatoes or capsicums could be stuffed (no pre-cooking required).

Preparation Plan
- steam onions; stuff and bake
- bake pumpkin
- prepare salad, and serve

Stuffed Onions

4 large onions	¼ cup mayonnaise or yoghurt
¾ cup tinned salmon, tuna or sardines	3 tbs finely chopped parsley
½ cup grated courgette	2 tbs finely chopped mint

Peel onions and steam for 10 minutes or more while preparing other ingredients and preparing pumpkin for baking. Preheat oven to 190ºC. Start baking pumpkin as soon as oven is heated.

Combine fish and remaining ingredients. Cut a slice off the top of each onion. Hollow out onion with a small spoon to leave a secure 5mm shell. Finely chop enough scooped-out onion to make ½ cup (reserve remainder for soup, sauces, etc). Stir into fish mixture and spoon into onion shells. Fit snugly into an oiled casserole dish and bake for about 20 minutes, until tender.

Spicy Pumpkin

pumpkin, halved and seeded	honey
lemon	mixed spice

Slice pumpkin into slim, even wedges. Place in one layer in an oiled pan. Drizzle with lemon juice and honey and sprinkle with mixed spice. Bake for 20 minutes or more until tender.

Tomato and Cabbage Salad

grated cabbage	¼ cup toasted pumpkin kernels
sliced tomatoes	1 tsp coriander
3 tbs cold-pressed oil	herb salt

Combine all the ingredients and toss well.

- *Eggplant Stuffed with Cornbread, Sage and Nuts* •
- *Onion Gravy* •
- *Courgette Salad* •

An Italy-meets-New England composition. Eggplants are halved (allow about two halves per person depending on size — of the eggplant and the persons); filled with a cornbread, sage and nut stuffing; braised in liquid which is thickened into gravy; and served with a crunchy salad. It is better to use many small, rather than a few large, eggplant as they will cook faster.

Preparation Plan
- stuff and braise eggplant
- prepare gravy
- prepare salad, and serve

Stuffed Eggplant

4 small-medium eggplant	½ tsp thyme
olive oil	½ tsp sage
2 sticks celery, chopped	herb salt
1 small green pepper, chopped	½ cup corn
¾ cup pecans, walnuts, almonds or	1½ cups crumbled gluten-free cornbread
other nuts	or other
1 tsp paprika	2 beaten eggs or ½ cup yoghurt

Preheat oven to 220ºC. Halve eggplant lengthwise. Hollow out the centre of each, leaving a secure 15mm shell. Chop the centre flesh finely. Brush insides with olive oil. Place shells in one layer in a deep, oiled baking pan. Place in oven to initiate cooking while preparing stuffing.

In olive oil fry chopped eggplant, celery, pepper and nuts for about 5 minutes until vegetables are soft but not brown. Fry in herbs and spices, then remove from heat. Stir in the remaining ingredients. Drizzle with olive oil and surround with braising liquid as outlined under Onion Gravy. Bake for 25 minutes or more until eggplant is very tender.

Onion Gravy

3 cups Vegetable Stock	1 tsp mixed herbs
1 large onion, sliced	1 tsp basil
3 tbs miso or marmite	½ tsp nutmeg
1 tbs molasses	4-6 tbs rice flour or other
3 tbs food yeast	

Place all the ingredients (they needn't be completely blended) — except rice flour — in the baking pan to surround eggplant. Bake as above.

About 5 minutes before serving time, drain off gravy and onions into a small saucepan. The eggplant may be removed to a heatproof platter and returned to the oven. Whisk flour into gravy and bring to the boil until desired thickness. Serve.

Courgette Salad

grated courgette	1 tsp honey
grated carrot	1 tsp mild curry powder
2 tbs cold-pressed oil	

Toss all the ingredients and serve.

- *Eggplant with Curried Vegetable Stuffing* •
- *Ginger Rice* •
- *Carrot Salad* •

An Indian-style stuffed eggplant dish and accompaniments.

Preparation Plan
- cook rice
- prepare eggplant
- prepare salad, and serve

Ginger Rice

2 cups brown rice
3¾ cups water
1 tbs chopped peeled ginger root

½ tsp turmeric
½ tsp allspice
herb salt

Bring all the ingredients to the boil, covered, and boil for 10 minutes. Turn off heat and cover top and sides of pot with a thick towel to trap in steam. Leave undisturbed for 20 minutes or more.

Eggplant with Curried Vegetable Stuffing

2 large or 4 small eggplant
3 tbs ghee or oil
¼ cup finely chopped onions
1 tsp finely chopped ginger root
1 tsp finely chopped garlic
herb salt
2 tsp coriander

1 tsp garam masala
¼ tsp chilli powder
½ cup chopped beans
½ cup peas
2 courgettes, finely chopped
2 medium tomatoes, chopped
3 tbs chopped parsley

Preheat oven to 200ºC. Slice eggplant in half lengthwise. Spoon out pulp from each to leave a 10mm shell. Chop the pulp finely.

Heat the ghee or oil over a medium heat and fry the garlic, ginger and onions for 2 minutes. Add seasonings and cook for one minute. Add eggplant pulp and cook for 5 minutes.

Stir in remaining ingredients, reduce heat to low, cover, and simmer for 5 minutes until tender.

Fill eggplant shells with mixture and place in one layer in an oiled casserole dish. Bake for 20 minutes or more until very tender.

Carrot Salad

2-3 large carrots, grated
few sliced radishes
3 tbs chopped mint

¼ cup lemon juice
¼ cup chopped dates

Combine all the ingredients, cover and chill until serving.

101   Pumpkin Buns & Salad   SERVES 4

- *Pumpkin Buns*
- *Sailor Salad*
- *Red Sky Dressing*

This bread recipe only squeaks by on the 40-minute limit if you already have the pumpkin cooked and mashed. Do it in the evening or the morning before going to work and you'll applaud yourself for the extra effort when you bite into these fabulous damper-style buns. The recipe doubles well — it may be prepared as two large loaves, and left-over bread can be frozen and later reheated to serve. Of course, instead of salad this can admirably accompany soup.

Preparation Plan
- cook and mash pumpkin; prepare buns
- prepare dressing
- prepare salad, and serve

Pumpkin Buns

4 cups flour (wheat is best)	30g butter or margarine
4 tsp baking powder	1½ cups mashed pumpkin
½ tsp salt	¼-⅓ cup water

Preheat oven to 200°C. Combine flour, baking powder and salt in a large bowl. Add pumpkin and enough water to make a sticky dough. On a lightly floured surface knead briefly until smooth.

Form dough into balls to almost fill large, greased muffin cups. Cut a cross in each and sprinkle with flour. Bake at 200°C for 10 minutes, then turn heat to 180°C and bake for about 10 minutes. Alternate position in oven during baking time.

Red Sky Dressing

1 cup Homemade Mayonnaise	2 tsp paprika
¼ cup tomato relish or ketchup	2 tsp curry powder

Combine all the ingredients.

Sailor Salad

small cauliflower segments	grated carrot
celery slices	sardines, salmon, tuna or fresh cooked fish
shredded cabbage	alfalfa sprouts

Combine all the ingredients (except sprouts). Toss with half the dressing (pass remainder) and arrange on platter. Surround with alfalfa sprouts.

- *Millet Herb Bread* •
- *Mushroom Sauce* •
- *Vegetable Medley* •

Squares of quick-to-bake millet bread are served with a topping of brightly coloured, steamed, mixed vegetables and a draping of mushroom sauce. A simple and popular meal — everyone is always impressed when there is hot bread on the table.

Preparation Plan

- bake bread
- prepare sauce
- prepare vegetables, and serve

Millet Herb Bread

1½ cups rice flour or other
½ cup ground millet
2 tbs honey
3 tsp baking powder or
   1 tbs Prepared Yeast
1 cup milk

¼ cup cold-pressed oil
1 egg
¼ cup chopped parsley
3 spring onions, chopped
½-1 tsp herb salt

Preheat oven to 220°C. Beat all ingredients vigorously for one minute. Pour into a 23cm-square, oiled pan. Bake for 20 minutes or until the centre springs back when lightly touched — do not overbake. Slice into squares and place on a serving platter. Top and surround with Vegetable Medley. Drizzle with sauce and pass remainder.

Mushroom Sauce

1 cup Vegetable Stock
1 cup milk (cow, soy, goat, coconut cream)
3 tbs rice flour or other
1½ tbs food yeast
6-8 sliced mushrooms
1 small onion, diced

2 bay leaves
1 clove garlic, chopped
1 tsp dill seed
¼ tsp nutmeg
herb salt

Combine all the ingredients in a saucepan and bring to the boil. Simmer for 10 minutes or more.

Vegetable Medley

whole baby carrots
asparagus or green beans
scallopini squash

brussels sprouts
1 tbs cold-pressed oil
2 tsp cumin powder

Keep the vegetables in large, possibly whole, pieces. Steam just until tender. Toss with oil and cumin.

- *Savoury Walnut Loaf* •
- *Tamarillo and Beet Chutney* •
- *Mashed Carrot* •

This is another excerpt from my childhood scrapbook of recipes. With alterations, of course, but still simple and yummy. The chutney can be served hot, cold or at room temperature.

Preparation Plan
- prepare loaf and bake
- prepare chutney
- steam and mash carrots, and serve

Savoury Walnut Loaf

2 eggs
1 cup ground walnuts
1 cup breadcrumbs
1 block tofu, mashed or
  1 cup cottage cheese

1 cup milk (cow, goat, soy, coconut cream)
¼ cup chopped parsley
3 tbs soy sauce
½ tsp nutmeg

Preheat oven to 190°C. Beat eggs and stir in the remaining ingredients. Pat into an oiled loaf pan or small casserole dish and bake for 20 minutes or until firm.

Tamarillo and Beet Chutney

4 tamarillos
1 large beetroot, cubed
1 small onion, chopped
¼ cup white wine or water
2 tbs apple cider vinegar
2 tbs brown sugar or honey

1 tbs prepared mustard
1 tbs marmite or miso
½ tsp dill or carraway seeds
¼ tsp bouquet garni
¼ tsp allspice

Scoop out the flesh of the tamarillo and coarsely chop. Place it with the remaining ingredients in a small saucepan. Bring to the boil and simmer, partly covered, for 15 minutes until thick, tender and flavourful.

Mashed Carrot

chopped carrots

Steam until tender. Drain and reserve liquid. Mash carrots with a potato masher, incorporating some of the hot reserved liquid, until of desired consistency.

- *Potato Babka* •
- *Steamed Spinach* •
- *Sesame Salad* •

A delicious homey Ukrainian puffed potato creation. The 40-minute timing is tight, so I give full preparation tips for speedy results.

Preparation Plan
- mash potato; prepare filling and bake
- toss salad
- steam spinach, and serve

Potato Babka

4 medium potatoes	¾ cup cottage cheese or mashed tofu or
3 eggs, separated	½ cup crumbled feta (cow, sheep, goat)
½ cup cream, coconut cream or	½ tsp turmeric
goat yoghurt	herb salt

Bring water to the boil. Scrub and chop potatoes into small pieces. Steam for 5 minutes until soft.

Meanwhile preheat oven to 220°C and grease an 8-cup casserole dish. Prepare the remaining ingredients.

Mash potatoes. Beat in egg yolks. Beat in cream, cheese and seasonings until light and fluffy. Beat egg whites until stiff. Gently fold into potato mixture. Pour into casserole dish and bake for 20-25 minutes until puffed and golden brown. Serve at once, directly from dish.

Sesame Salad

3 tbs sesame seeds	Dressing:
	3 tbs cold-pressed oil
grated cabbage	1 tbs natural soy sauce
celery, chopped	1 tsp honey
raw peas	1 tsp mild curry powder
radishes, chopped	

Toast sesame seeds and combine with the dressing ingredients. Toss with the vegetables. Keep covered until serving time.

Steamed Spinach

spinach or silverbeet

Break into large pieces and steam for 3-5 minutes until tender. Serve.

- *Potato Burgers* •
- *Burger Filling* •
- *Crunchy Salad* •

A similar concept to Potato Parcels, but with a few magic touches something original is born. Here potatoes are baked, topped with tomato and sesame seeds, split horizontally leaving a secure hinge at one end, and filled with a hearty mushroom sauce and vegetable mixture. Serve with a colourful crunchy salad.

Preparation Plan

- cook potatoes
- prepare filling
- prepare salad, and serve

Potato Burgers

4-8 large potatoes	basil
1-2 large firm tomatoes	freshly ground pepper
sesame seeds	

Bake potatoes (or roast in an electric frypan) at 190ºC until almost done — for about 25 minutes. Top each one with a large slice of tomato. Sprinkle with sesame seeds, basil and pepper. Bake until done. Split horizontally as outlined above and serve filled to overflowing.

Burger Filling

3 cups Vegetable Stock	1 tsp chopped garlic
6 tbs rice flour or other	1 cup corn
3 tbs natural soy sauce	1 large onion, sliced
1 tsp dry mustard	½ cup mushrooms, sliced
1 tsp paprika	1-2 blocks tofu, cubed
1 tsp curry powder	or 4 hard-boiled eggs, chopped
1 tsp oreganum	or 1½ cups mince

Bring all the ingredients to the boil and simmer for 15 minutes or more until tender and flavourful.

Crunchy Salad

grated beetroot	½ cup pineapple pieces
grated carrot	2 tsp curry powder
grated cabbage	½ tsp paprika
1 cup Homemade Mayonnaise or yoghurt	¼ tsp nutmeg

Arrange concentric circles of grated vegetables on a serving platter. Combine the remaining ingredients and drizzle over salad.

- *Paella* •
- *Raw Vegetable Platter* •

Paella (pie-ay-yuh) is a classic Spanish rice dish served in a myriad of ways but commonly containing seafood, spicy sausage and chicken pieces. For more special presentation procede with a garlicky finger-licking antipasto and omit the crudites. This is one of my favourite dishes and perfect for casual entertaining, so I didn't resist including it despite the one-hour overall timing. Preparation is actually quick but it requires 35 minutes baking time and 5 minutes resting time before serving.

Preparation Plan
- fry seafood and rice; bake
- slice vegetables, and serve

Paella

¼ cup olive oil	1 tsp thyme
½ cup chopped onions	1 tsp herb salt
1 red or green pepper, in strips	
400g spicy sausage, in thin rounds (optional)	3 cups brown rice
	5½ cups boiling water
2 cups squid rings	12 olives, chopped
400g fish in medium chunks	1 cup peas or chopped beans
1 tsp finely chopped garlic	
1 tsp paprika	12 or more mussels in shells
½ tsp turmeric or	lemon wedges
¼ tsp ground saffron	

Preheat oven to 200°C.

In olive oil fry onions, peppers and sausage for 5 minutes. Stir in squid, fish, garlic and seasonings, and cook for about 3 minutes until well coloured.

Add rice and cook for 3 minutes until well coloured. Add water, olives and peas, and bring to a rolling boil. Stir so that squid and fish are mostly on top and scatter the mussels over top. Immediately place on the bottom of the oven. Do not stir at any point. Bake uncovered for 35 minutes.

Remove from the oven and cover with a towel. Let rest for 5-8 minutes. Garnish with lemon wedges and serve.

Raw Vegetable Platter

thin carrot slices	tomato wedges
angle-cut celery segments	basil or chives

Arrange vegetables in rows on a rectangular platter and sprinkle with fresh or dried basil or fresh chopped chives.

- *Mexicana Chicken or Fish/Seafood or Tofu/Tempeh* •
- *Poppyseed Pasta or Corn Chips* •
- *Salsa Salad* •

This is easy enough to cook for one or exotic enough for entertaining. Remember the sauce topping for vegetables, rice or beans. And no messy pots to clean!

Preparation Plan
- prepare and bake chicken or option
- cook pasta
- prepare salad; toss noodles, and serve

Mexicana Chicken

2 x ¼ segments chicken

Topping:
1 small carrot, diced
1 small onion, diced
1 small courgette, diced
6 olives (optional)
4 cloves garlic, chopped

½ cup tomato puree
2 tsp each: molasses
  natural soy sauce
  brown sugar or honey
  oreganum
  cumin powder
  paprika
½ tsp cinnamon

Preheat oven to 200°C.

Place each chicken segment on a large sheet of aluminium foil. Combine the remaining ingredients and spread over the chicken. Wrap the foil securely to be airtight and place in a baking dish keeping the chicken pieces in one layer (if cooking extra chicken wrap no more than one piece in each foil parcel or this disturbs the time/heat ratio).

Bake for 40 minutes (for even more flavour and less preparation time at dinner, prepare and wrap the chicken in the morning and bake later). Remove foil before serving and "stir" topping to refresh colour.

---

or Mexicana Whole Fish

Prepare as above. Bake for 25-30 minutes.

---

or Mexicana Fish Fillets/Seafood or Tofu/Tempeh

Combine topping as above. Bring to the boil and simmer for 20 minutes or longer. Add fish fillets, squid rings, mussels, or cubes of tofu or tempeh. Simmer gently for 10 minutes or more, adding wine or Vegetable Stock to thin if necessary.

Poppyseed Pasta

large shell-shaped pasta
1 tbs cold-pressed oil
1 tbs poppyseeds

2 tsp natural soy sauce
1 tsp basil

Cook pasta according to packet instructions. Drain and toss with the remaining ingredients.

Salsa Salad

2 tbs apple cider vinegar
2 tsp honey
2 tbs fresh chopped mint or
  lemon balm or dill

1 large tomato, diced
½ cup cubed cucumber
½ red pepper, diced

Thoroughly combine all the ingredients. Cover and allow to sit for at least 10 minutes.

- *Chinese 5-Dragon Whole Fish or Vegetarian or Liver or Soy Kebabs* •
  - *Lemon Rice* •
- *Sesame Spinach Salad* •

This is superb and ready in minutes. Fillets of fish may be used but whole fish is cheaper and makes an impressive entrance onto the table. The fish or rice could include many more vegetables, or prepare the sauce on its own and serve it over vegetables, rice, beans or pasta.

Preparation Plan
- cook rice
- cook fish or option
- prepare salad, and serve

Lemon Rice

1½ cups brown rice	grated rind of 1 lemon
2¾ cups water, stock or orange juice	same lemon sliced and chopped
½ tsp turmeric	herb salt

Bring all the ingredients to the boil, and boil covered and undisturbed for 10 minutes. Turn heat off and cover top and sides of pot with a thick towel to trap in heat. Let sit undisturbed for 25 minutes or longer.

Chinese 5-Dragon Whole Fish

1 kg whole fish, gutted and scaled	1 tbs cold-pressed oil
	2 tsp cumin powder
Sauce:	2 tsp honey
1 cup pineapple juice	1 tsp powdered ginger or
½ cup pineapple pieces	1 tsp peeled, chopped ginger root
1½ tbs natural soy sauce	1 tsp Chinese 5-spice powder

Place fish in an electric frypan or heavy large frypan or pot. Combine all the Sauce ingredients and pour over fish, turning to coat evenly. Simmer for 20 minutes, turning and basting occasionally. Serve whole on a platter and slice at the table.

or Chinese 5-Dragon Vegetarian or Fish or Liver or Soy Kebabs

double the Sauce ingredients above	¾ cup sunflower seed kernels, pumpkin
4 tbs rice flour or 3 tbs arrowroot	kernels and/or peanuts (optional)

Combine the Sauce ingredients with flour. Bring to the boil and simmer for 10 minutes or more. On bamboo skewers thread chicken livers, fish cubes, mussels, or cubes of tofu or tempeh along with a selection of vegetables such as courgette, eggplant slices, mushroom, baby tomatoes, onion, green pepper. Grill for about 5 minutes on each side. Serve on a platter teepee style and drizzle with some of the sauce; pass the remainder.

If using the all-Vegetarian option, toast the nuts and seeds and sprinkle over the kebabs.

Sesame Spinach Salad

spinach leaves	1 tbs cold-pressed oil
Dressing:	1 tsp coriander
2 tbs sesame seeds	½ tsp Chinese 5-spice powder

Combine the dressing ingredients. Leave spinach leaves whole or break in half; toss with dressing. Arrange on a platter.

A Little Something Extra

APPETISERS

Any of the homey menus in this book can be presented with more attention to artistic detail, and accompanied by a quickly made first course and later a dessert, to metamorphose into entrancingly elegant dining.

An appetiser should be what the name suggests and stimulate — rather than satiate — the appetite. So think light, and think visual.

---

109 Melon and Port

melon   smoked ham or black figs
port

Serve scoops of melon in long stemmed glasses and drizzle each serving with 1-2 tablespoons Port. Cut a triangular slice of melon with rind and secure on each glass rim. With a cocktail toothpick pierce through the melon while also securing a tiny roll of ham or half a black fig.

---

110 Avocado Cream

avocado   cooked fish roe or toasted cashews
radishes   spring onions
sour cream or Savoury Tofu Whip

On small plates arrange slices of avocado. On one side place a large radish. To decorate radishes cut almost to the base making a series of parallel thin slices. Slice again at right angles almost to the base. Combine cream with fish roe and onions. Dollop over avocado.

---

111 Mountain Mushrooms

large mushrooms (about 3 per person)   Chinese 5-spice powder
cream cheese and yoghurt or   soy sauce
   Savoury Tofu Whip   cucumber
toasted sesame seeds   paprika

Remove stems from mushrooms. Combine 2 parts cream cheese to one part yoghurt or use all tofu. Stir in seeds, spice and soy sauce to taste. Fill each mushroom cap. Stud with tiny cucumber slices and sprinkle with paprika.

---

112   *Tomato Flowers*

tomatoes (1 per person)
Vinaigrette
walnuts

parmesan or grilled cubes of tofu
   drizzled with soy sauce

Make 2 vertical cuts at right angles to each other, almost to the base of each tomato, creating four equal "petals". Combine vinaigrette with nuts and cheese or option to taste. Place tomatoes on a bed of shredded lettuce and dollop with dressing over the centre of each tomato.

113   *Mussel Builders*

Homemade Mayonnaise
paprika
garlic or chilli mussels, chopped
  (available from deli)

curry powder
whole lettuce
baby tomatoes (1 per person)

Combine mayonnaise with paprika, curry and mussels. Slice lettuce in half, then slice 2-3 thin wedges per person. Fan out wedges on each plate and garnish with a baby tomato. Dollop lettuce with mussel dressing.

114   *Stuffed Grapes*

large black grapes
cream cheese, softened or

stiff Savoury Tofu Whip
finely chopped salted nuts

Split each grape and remove seeds with the point of a knife. Use a piping bag or spoon to place cream cheese in each grape, allowing filling to come well above the top of the grape. Dip top in nuts. Serve or chill.

115   *Pears in Tarragon Cream*

ripe or tinned pears
blue cheese, goat-camembert or
   chopped toasted nuts
lettuce leaves

Homemade Mayonnaise
tarragon
fresh dill
paprika

Peel, core and halve pears. Combine cheese or option with a little mayonnaise and fill pear cavities. Place one half cut-side down on a lettuce leaf on each serving plate.

Combine mayonnaise with tarragon and fresh dill to taste (for a richer topping use half mayonnaise, half whipped cream). Pour a few tablespoons over each pear to cover. Sprinkle with paprika, chill or serve.

116　*Bouquet of Asparagus*　SERVES 4

asparagus
6 tbs cold-pressed oil
2 tbs apple cider vinegar
2 tsp honey
1-2 cloves garlic, chopped
1 tsp grated lemon peel
1 tsp tarragon

herb salt
freshly ground pepper
1 large red pepper, sliced for maximum
　　length of slices
rye toast or rice crackers (optional)
butter and miso (optional)

Steam asparagus. Combine other ingredients and pour over asparagus; toss. Chill, stirring occasionally, for an hour or longer. Arrange a few spears on each plate and tie loosely with a long strand of red pepper.

May be served with small triangles of dark rye bread spread with butter and miso.

117　*Antipasto*

celery
mushrooms
broccoli
cauliflower
carrots
peppers
tomato
courgette
cucumber

bean sprouts
options: olives,
　　mussels, oysters,
　　sardines, anchovies,
　　pickled vegetables,
　　cornchips
curry yoghurt dip
sesame seed Savoury Tofu Whip
garlic Homemade Mayonnaise

There is great scope for inventiveness. On one large serving plate arrange in concentric circles, or radiating spokes, a selection of raw vegetables and other accompaniments. At the centre or to one side place a bowl of dip or dressing.

118　*Baby Corn Consomme*　SERVES 6-8

4½ cups Vegetable (or meat) Stock
2 cups pureed tomatoes
3 tbs apple cider vinegar
1 tbs honey
3 tbs soy sauce
3 tbs food yeast

1 tsp Chinese 5-spice
1 tsp curry powder
1 tsp mixed herbs
1 tin baby ears of corn
2-3 spring onions

Bring all the ingredients (except spring onions) to the boil. Simmer for 20 minutes or longer. Garnish with chopped spring onions.

As a luxurious garnish, one or more scallops per person may be briefly simmered in the soup.

119 *Gazpacho*

1 cup fresh breadcrumbs
3 tbs olive oil
3 tbs apple cider vinegar
1 cup ice-cold water
6 large ripe tomatoes
1 medium cucumber, peeled

1 small onion
1-3 cloves garlic
herb salt
freshly ground pepper
few drops tabasco or chilli sauce

Have all the vegetables chilled. Soak breadcrumbs in oil and vinegar while coarsely chopping all the vegetables. Whizz in a blender the vegetables, breadcrumbs, water and seasonings until well pureed. Add more breadcrumbs or water depending on desired consistency.

This is best chilled for up to 2 hours but may be served immediately in chilled bowls with a few ice-cubes, made with tomato puree or a slice of lemon set in each cube.

Serve with more chopped cucumber or croutons as a garnish.

120 *Fish in Lemon Cups* SERVES 4

2 large well-shaped lemons
¾ cup cream or
   ½ cup Homemade Mayonnaise and
   ½ cup yoghurt or
   Savoury Tofu Whip
2 tsp mild curry powder

1 tsp basil
100g tinned salmon or cooked roe or
  smoked fish
½ cup peeled cucumber in small cubes
paprika

Slice the lemons in half crosswise. Carefully squeeze out juice, then remove any flesh. Trim base of cups so they stand securely. Whip the cream with the lemon juice, basil and curry powder (or combine these ingredients with the cream option). Strain the liquid from the salmon, mash fish with a fork and stir into cream with the cucumber. Place in shells and garnish with a few small triangles of cucumber with peel on; dust with paprika.

DESSERTS

You'd love to serve your guests an exciting dessert but there isn't time? Read on and note the many options to despair: desserts which are light to eat, simple to prepare and stunning to serve.

When whipped cream or any other creamy accompaniment or topping is suggested, any of the following may be used:
- Sweet Tofu Whip
- Lite Licks (soy milk ice-"cream")
- Goat's Milk Ice-creams
- New American All-Natural Ice-creams
- Yoghurt or sour cream, or cream cheese blended with yoghurt

---

121 Sweet Tofu Whip

An easy foundational element to many recipes, and a delight to eat on its own, with fruit as a simple dessert, or as a nourishing protein and calcium-rich breakfast. Covered and refrigerated it keeps well for several days.

1 block (1 cup) tofu
¼-½ cup fruit juice
1 ripe banana
3 tbs honey
2 tbs cold-pressed oil

flavour variations:
    coconut, dried fruit, fresh fruit,
    nuts, seeds, natural essences,
    mixed spice, cinnamon,
    grated ginger root

Whizz all the ingredients in a blender or food processor. Thin if necessary with more fruit juice. Add one or more flavour variations as desired.

---

122 Piped Sweet Tofu Whip

Remember that the whip needs to be as thick and firm as possible or it won't hold its shape. Also do not add any flavour variations like coconut or bits of fruit which will clog the piping nozzles.

1 small block tofu
2 tbs cold-pressed oil
3 tbs honey

dash vanilla
pinch cinnamon or nutmeg

Whizz all the ingredients in a blender. Chill for 20-60 minutes or longer to firm. Fill piping bag and use for garnishes (for savoury uses — omit vanilla and spices).

---

123 *Glazed Strawberry Flan* SERVES 6-8

• *30 minutes preparation time* •
• *20-40 minutes chilling time* •

This is colourfully inviting with fresh berries, but kiwifruit, a banana and grape combination, or even stewed winter fruit may be used. This stores well overnight or otherwise needs a 40-minute chilling time in the fridge or 20 minutes in the freezer.

Base

3½ tbs butter or oil
1 tbs honey

2 tbs raw sugar
2 cups rice bubbles or toasted muesli

Melt butter, honey and sugar, and bring to the boil. Simmer for 5 minutes. Stir in rice bubbles or muesli and press into a 20cm circle onto a large serving plate. Chill while preparing topping.

Cream Cheese or Tofu Filling

250g cream cheese
¼ cup orange juice
1 tbs icing sugar

1 tsp pure vanilla
(or instead of the above a firm
Sweet Tofu Whip may be used)

Whizz all the ingredients in a blender until smooth. Pour over chilled base. Chill while preparing Berries and Cream, and Glaze.

Berries and Cream

500g fresh strawberries, hulled,
washed and drained

unsweetened whipped cream or
Tofu Whip for Piping

Use whole berries and place point side up onto cream cheese filling.

Glaze

¼ cup strawberry jam

1 tbs water

Stir over a low heat for 2-3 minutes until smooth. Pour over strawberries using a pastry brush to cover each berry. Chill for 40 minutes or more in the refrigerator, or 20 minutes or more in the freezer.

124 *Tropical Cream Pie*

- *30 minutes preparation time* •
- *30 minutes chilling time* •

A light creamy potpourri of crispy cookie crust, banana-apricot filling, and coconut-pineapple-rum-cream topping. And ready in a tropical breeze. For faster chilling time use your freezer.

Cookie Crust

1¾ cups crushed wholemeal or
  gluten-free cookies (200g packet)

4 tbs butter or margarine
3 tbs carob or 2 tbs cocoa powder

Melt butter and stir in cookie crumbs and carob or cocoa. Pat into a 23cm pie plate. Chill.

Banana-Apricot Filling

2 cups apricot juice
½ cup diced dried apricots

2½ tsp agar granules
2 large bananas, well chopped

Bring half the apricot juice, apricots and agar to the boil. Boil for one minute. Remove from heat and stir in banana and remaining apricot juice. To cool place saucepan in a bowl or sink of cold water; stir occasionally to keep from completely setting.

While cooling prepare cream topping. As soon as filling is close to room temperature or almost set, pour onto chilled crust and refrigerate.

Tropical Cream Topping

300ml cream or use
  Sweet Tofu Whip omitting honey
3 tbs brown sugar
3 tbs rum to taste

or 1 tsp pure vanilla
⅓ cup chopped pineapple pieces
2 tbs candied ginger, diced (optional)
¼ cup coconut

Beat cream, brown sugar and rum until almost stiff. Fold in pineapple and ginger. Pour over filled crust. Chill for 30 minutes or longer.

Toast coconut in a sturdy frypan until lightly browned — watch carefully. Use to garnish pie: place small circles of coconut around top edge of pie and stud with an apricot half.

- *30 minutes preparation time*
- *30 minutes chilling time*

Wonderfully open to seasonal variation, this is a whizz to prepare. A cookie crust, creamy filling and concentric circles of fresh fruit with a quick agar glaze.

Cookie Crust

80g butter or margarine
1 cup crushed cookies

¾ cup coconut or finely ground nuts

Melt butter and stir in crumbs and coconut or nuts. Press onto bottom and 3cm up the sides of a 23cm springform pan. Chill while preparing filling.

Creamy Filling

300ml cream
4 tbs icing sugar
1 tsp vanilla
grated peel of 1 lemon

250g sour cream
or omit creams and use
2½ cups Sweet Tofu Whip

Whip cream with sugar, vanilla and lemon peel. Fold in sour cream (or Tofu Whip using lemon peel and juice in its preparation).

Pour onto crust and chill while preparing fruit.

Fruit

3 or more seasonal fruits such as: banana, orange, kiwifruit

Slice fruit attractively and place in concentric circles on top of pie. Chill while preparing glaze.

Sweet Agar Glaze

1 cup water
2 tsp sugar

1 tsp agar granules

Bring all the ingredients to the boil.

Pour over fruit to cover. Chill pie for 10 minutes or more until set.

126 *Apricot Ginger Mousse* SERVES 8-10

• *20-30 minutes preparation time* •
• *1 hour chilling time* •

This is light and sensuous and can be served in individual glasses (with briefer chilling time) or one large glass bowl. If you don't like ginger try adding toasted almonds or long strands of toasted coconut. Instead of the usual whipped cream on top there is a quick and gossamer meringue.

2½ cups fresh (or soaked, dried)
   apricot pieces
2½ cups apricot juice
¼ cup margarine or butter or oil
6 egg yolks
6 tbs arrowroot
2 tbs gelatine
1-3 tbs chopped candied ginger
¼ tsp nutmeg

1 tsp vanilla
5 egg whites
6 tbs icing sugar

Meringue Topping:
1 egg white
1 tbs icing sugar
thin slices of apricot
   for decoration

Bring apricots, juice, margarine, egg yolks, arrowroot, gelatine, ginger and nutmeg to the boil. Boil for one minute stirring constantly. Remove from heat and stir in vanilla.

Cool the mixture quickly by placing the saucepan in a bowl or sink full of cold water. Once the custard comes to room temperature, refrigerate for about 30 minutes until mixture begins to mound when dropped from a spoon.

Then beat the egg whites until frothy. Gradually add icing sugar and beat until very stiff. Lightly but thoroughly fold into custard. Pour into individual dishes or one large glass dish and chill until firm, for 30 minutes or longer.

No more than one hour before serving beat the egg white until frothy, then beat in the icing sugar until very stiff. Place a spoonful of the meringue on each serving and top with 2 thin slices of apricot.

• *30 minutes preparation time* •
• *20 minutes or more chilling time* •

Two simple fillings — one carob, coffee and hazelnut; one a quick fluffy meringue — are layered in decorative glasses. Rich in taste, light in texture and kilojoules, these morsels perfectly punctuate an elegant dinner.

Mocha Nut Filling

2 cups boiling water
3 tbs carob powder
4 tsp cereal coffee
½ tsp cinnamon
4 egg yolks
3 tbs rice flour

1 tsp agar granules
4 tbs brown sugar
4 tbs margarine or butter
1 tsp vanilla
½ cup hazelnuts

Dissolve carob, coffee and cinnamon in boiling water. Place in a double boiler over boiling water and beat in eggs, flour, sugar and agar. Cook until thick and bubbling — for about 5 minutes.

Place in a sink of cold water, stir in margarine and vanilla, and cool to lukewarm.

While preparing the Meringue, toast the hazelnuts. Chop, then add half to Mocha Filling and reserve half for garnishing.

Fluffy Meringue

4 egg whites
6 tbs icing sugar

1 tsp vanilla

Beat egg whites until stiff, then gradually beat in sugar and vanilla until very stiff.

Once the Mocha Filling is cool, layer in glasses in this order: Mocha, Meringue, Mocha, Meringue, nuts. Chill for 20 minutes or up to one hour — any longer and the meringue subsides.

128 *Parisian Parfaits* Serves any number

- *10-20 minutes preparation time* •
- *Up to 15 minutes chilling time* •

Obviously anything goes with this sort of layered construction but two delicious variations are outlined: Lemon-Raspberry and Apple-Prune Parfaits.

Lemon-Raspberry Parfaits

yoghurt and cream cheese
  or Sweet Tofu Whip
fresh or stewed or soaked dried fruit
cubes of cake or crumbled cookies
nuts

carob-covered raisins
chopped carob bars

fun fruit garnishes

Whizz in a blender a mixture of half yoghurt and half cream cheese, lemon juice and grated rind, and icing sugar or honey to taste. Layer in decorative glasses with fresh or tinned raspberries or other colourful fruit. Chill briefly if possible (or overnight) and garnish just before serving.

Garnish: on rim of glass secure one round slice of lemon. Make a slit at the top under the skin. Cut a long thin flexible strip of lemon rind from another slice and place this through the slit; tie into a jaunty knot.

Apple-Prune Parfaits

Sweet Tofu Whip
pitted prunes
mixed spice

stewed apple
walnuts or brazils
few apple slices

In decorative glasses layer Sweet Tofu Whip (which has been flavoured with chopped prunes and mixed spice) and stewed apple mixed with walnuts or chopped, toasted brazils. Chill; garnish just before serving.

Garnish: Secure an unpeeled circular slice of apple on the rim and pierce it through a cocktail toothpick holding a prune.

129 *Apple Snow*

• 20 minutes preparation time •
• Up to several hours chilling or freezing time •

This is a classic Scandinavian dessert. It may be served immediately, chilled for a few hours, or frozen and served as an ice. Garnish lavishly with fresh fruit and perhaps a few crisp homemade cookies.

---

2 cups fresh hulled strawberries or
   2 cups tart applesauce
4 egg whites
½ cup sugar
pinch of salt

½ tsp lemon juice
1 cup whipped cream or
   stiff Sweet Tofu Whip
berries, black figs or
   other fresh fruit garnish

Whizz berries in a blender until pureed. Beat egg whites and salt until foamy. Gradually beat in sugar until whites are very stiff.

In a separate bowl combine the berry puree or applesauce with the lemon juice. Stir in a heaped tablespoon of egg white to lighten the mixture. Gently fold the remaining whites into the mixture, then gently fold in cream or option.

Serve as outlined above. The apple snow may be sprinkled with cinnamon.

---

130 *Melon Nests*

• 10-15 minutes preparation time •

Fresh seasonal fruit is ever an attractive finale. Think of subtle, simple ways in which it can be enhanced. Here chilled melon halves are filled with fresh berries and crumbled macaroons or brandy snaps. Then top with whipped cream or other option and lots of toasted, slivered almonds and long shreds of coconut.

½ melon per person
fresh berries
cakey-style macaroons or
   brandy snaps, crumbled

whipped cream or other option
toasted slivered almonds and
   long coconut shreds

Chill melons before preparing. Cut them in half, scoop out seeds and fill with berries and macaroon mixture. Top as above.

131 *Macaroon Peaches* *SERVES 6*

- *15-20 minutes preparation time* •
- *20-25 minutes baking time* •

This light fruity finale is of Italian derivation. If you want to be extravagant serve the peaches with custard laced with Marsala, a fortified wine like sherry.

6 firm, ripe peaches
6 cakey macaroons, crushed
  (1 cup crumbs)
2 tbs honey

4 tbs butter or margarine
2 egg yolks
Marsala custard or
  other creamy topping

Wash, halve and pit peaches. Scoop enough pulp out of each half to make a deep space in the centre yet leave the shell stable. Add this pulp to the macaroons, then stir in the honey, butter and egg yolks. Stuff each half with the mixture.

Arrange the halves side-by-side in a well-buttered oven dish or heatproof platter. Bake at 190ºC for 20-25 minutes, just until tender. Baste with the syrup produced in the pan during baking. Serve hot or cold with custard or other topping.

132 *English Berry Pudding* *SERVES 6-8*

- *15 minutes preparation time* •
- *12 hours chilling time* •

You could hardly have fewer ingredients or simpler construction. The mould comes out dripping with fruit syrup and deep red colour.

1.8kg fresh ripe berries
½ cup icing sugar
10-12 slices dense, homemade-style
  white bread

ample whipped cream or
  other creamy topping
a few berries for garnishing

Combine the fruit and sugar until the sugar is dissolved.

Cut a circle of bread to fit the bottom of a pudding basin or bowl. Trim the remaining slices to evenly and attractively fit around the inner surface of the mould, overlapping them by 5mm.

Ladle the fruit mixture inside the bread-lined mould and cover completely with the remaining bread. Cover the mould with a plate and place a weight or heavy pan on top. Chill for at least 12 hours until the bread is completely saturated with the syrup.

Invert onto a chilled serving plate. Decorate the base with piped whipped cream or option and stud with a few fresh berries.

133   *Marmalade Pudding*   SERVES 6

- *15 minutes preparation time*
- *40 minutes baking time*

A real homey Anglo-Saxon classic. Yummy, filling spongey pudding with a never-fail custard made without added sugar or milk.

Marmalade Pudding

1 cup chunky-style orange marmalade	1 tsp cinnamon
2 eggs	½ tsp nutmeg
4 tbs butter or margarine, softened	½ cup honey
1 cup rice flour or other	¼ cup milk (cow, goat, soy, coconut cream)
1½ tsp baking powder	¼ cup water
1 tsp powdered ginger	coarsely chopped peel from ½ large orange

Preheat the oven to 180°C. Over a low heat slowly melt the marmalade. Grease a 4-cup (preferably round), heat-proof bowl or casserole dish.

Whizz eggs in a blender until pale and thick. Add the remaining ingredients and whizz until blended.

Pour the hot marmalade into the greased bowl. Pour the batter on top and bake for 40 minutes until a toothpick inserted in the centre tests clean.

Cool the pudding in the pan for 10 minutes. Then run a knife along the side, place a hot plate over the top and invert. Serve warm accompanied with custard.

Apple Juice Custard

2 cups apple juice (preferably the cloudy, old-fashioned type)	2 tbs oil or butter or margarine
4 tbs rice flour	¼ tsp nutmeg
2 tbs honey	2 eggs
	1 tsp vanilla

While pudding is baking, bring the juice, flour, honey, oil and nutmeg to the boil. Meanwhile beat eggs and vanilla. Once custard has boiled and is thickened, beat about half cup of it into the beaten egg mixture to heat the eggs (this prevents curdling). Turn off the heat and beat the hot egg mixture into the saucepan. The mixture should be thick and creamy. Serve hot (also good cold for other desserts).

Carob Coffee Crisp

- *30 minutes preparation time* •
- *1 hour baking time* •

Two crisp, puffy carob and hazelnut meringue layers are covered with a cream or Tofu Whip and coffee blend, then stacked. Simple to make and enjoyed by everyone. Sprinkle around the top a ring of chopped carob bar, hazelnuts and coffee. Serve with dandelion coffee.

Meringues

6 egg whites	6 tbs carob powder
½ tsp cream of tartar	2 tsp vanilla
1¼ cups raw sugar	¾ cup roasted hazelnuts, finely chopped

Line one or two large baking trays with brown paper or foil. Draw two 23cm circles and grease thoroughly with butter or liquid lecithin.

Beat the egg whites with cream of tartar until stiff. Gradually beat in sugar and carob, beating for 10 minutes until very stiff. Fold in the vanilla and nuts. Spread the mixture evenly over the two circles. Bake at 140°C for one hour. Turn off oven and leave meringues for 2-3 hours or overnight.

Peel off paper and place one circle on a serving plate. Cover with half the Coffee Cream, the remaining Meringue and Cream. Sprinkle with an inner ring of the Topping and chill until ready to serve. Don't fill until four hours before serving or the meringue could lose its crispness.

Coffee Cream

600ml cream or	2 tbs cereal coffee
4 cups thick Sweet Tofu Whip	4 tbs honey (omit if using Sweet Tofu Whip)
6 tbs carob powder	1 tsp cinnamon

Whip cream with the remaining ingredients until fluffy. If using Tofu, whisk in remaining ingredients or whizz in a blender.

Mocha Nut Topping

2 small carob and nut bars	1 tsp cereal coffee granules
¼ cup roasted hazelnuts, finely chopped	

Chop the carob bars fine-medium. Stir in the remaining ingredients.

135 *Greek Coffee Cake*

• *10-20 minutes preparation time* •

So good and so simple. For an even lighter dessert forget the cake base and just have the grilled banana with coffee-syrup, perhaps a sprinkle of toasted hazelnuts and your choice of topping.

good quality purchased carrot cake or other
banana, raw or grilled or fried in
   butter until soft and dark
   or soaked dried apricots
chopped toasted hazelnuts (optional)

cereal-coffee
honey
cinnamon
coffee liqueur
whipped cream or option

In each individual dessert bowl place a square or round piece of cake. Combine prepared, strong cereal-coffee with honey, cinnamon, and coffee liqueur to taste. Pour a few tablespoons over each cake to soak. Top with choice of fruit and a little more "syrup". Either top or cover sides of dessert with piped whipped cream or option.

Instead of using fruit in the dessert, your choice of topping could be flavoured with chopped roasted hazelnuts and a sprinkle of coffee powder.

- *20 minutes preparation time* •
- *30-35 minutes baking time* •

Dense, moist fudgey slices dotted with creamy banana. Instead of dessert slices these can of course be sliced for snacks. For sweeter tastes, or for serving without the topping, you might wish to drizzle on a chocolate or carob glaze.

3 large eggs	4 tbs cocoa or
¾ cup cold-pressed oil	6 tbs carob powder
½ cup brown sugar	¾ cup chopped walnuts
⅓ cup honey	2-3 bananas, sliced
1 tsp pure vanilla	cinnamon
¾ cup rice flour or other	your choice of topping

Thoroughly beat the eggs. Beat in the oil, sugar, honey and vanilla. Beat in the flour, cocoa or carob, and nuts.

Pour into an oiled 20cm square pan. Top thickly with banana slices and sprinkle with cinnamon. Bake at 180°C for 30-35 minutes until centre tests done with a toothpick. Serve hot or cold with your choice of topping.

Cocoa or Carob Glaze (optional)

2 tbs honey	¼ tsp cinnamon
2 tbs cold-pressed oil	¾ cup milk powder (soy, goat or cow)
2 tbs cocoa or	1-3 tbs prepared cereal-coffee to thin
3 tbs carob powder	

Blend together honey, oil, cocoa or carob powder, and cinnamon. Blend in milk powder, adding sufficient liquid (in this case prepared coffee) to thin to desired consistency.

Remember this recipe for other uses, adding coffee powder, ground nuts, coconut, ginger, citrus peel, soaked dried fruit, etc for a number of delicious variations.

137 *Apple Ginger Slice*

- *25 minutes preparation time* •
- *25 minutes baking time* •

Ambrosia for ginger fanciers. A light cakey base supports sweet apple slices and spunky ginger glaze. May be served with lemon-flavoured Sweet Tofu Whip or whipped cream or other option.

Base

2 large eggs
¼ cup honey
¼ cup cold-pressed oil
1 tsp vanilla
1¼ cups rice flour or other

½ cup ground nuts
1 tsp powdered ginger
2 tsp grated lemon peel
2 apples, cored and thinly sliced

Thoroughly beat eggs. Beat in honey, oil and vanilla. Beat in flour, nuts, ginger and lemon peel. Pour into an oiled 20cm square pan and top with apple slices.

Bake at 180°C for 25-30 minutes. While warm cover with Ginger Glaze. Cool and slice.

Ginger Glaze

3 tbs honey
1 tbs cold-pressed oil
  or melted butter

3 tbs lemon juice
¾-1 cup milk powder (soy, goat or cow)
1-3 tbs diced candied ginger

Combine honey, oil and lemon juice. Beat in milk powder until of thick but still runny consistency. Stir in ginger to taste.

138 *Dipped Ice Bombe* SERVES ANY NUMBER

- *15-20 minutes preparation time* •
- *10-40 minutes chilling time* •

Serve this in individual dessert bowls (these have a briefer chilling time if that is important) or as a giant bombe. Make it with soy, goat's or cow's milk ice-cream and top it with a rich all-over draping of chocolate or carob topping. Serve with piped whipped cream or Sweet Tofu Whip for piping around the bottom edge and stud with fresh berries or toasted whole nuts.

Ice-Cream

1-3 flavours ice-cream
whipped cream or tofu for piping

berries, nuts or other garnish

In each individual dessert bowl meld together up to three flavours of ice-cream to create a smooth dome. Keep frozen while forming the next one.

To make one large bombe, place ice-cream in layers or alternating scoops in a round plastic or stainless steel bowl. Freeze until firm — 20 minutes or more. Meanwhile prepare Topping.

Topping (enough for 25cm bombe)

Chocolate Topping:
200g cooking chocolate
½ cup cream

Carob Topping:
3 tbs honey

2-3 tbs prepared, strong cereal-coffee
1 tbs cold-pressed oil or
  melted butter
¾ cup milk powder (soy, goat or cow)
4 tbs carob powder
½ tsp cinnamon

Chocolate Topping: Melt chocolate over simmering water. Remove from heat and stir in cream. Allow to cool without setting.

Carob Topping: Blend together honey, coffee and oil. Blend in milk and carob powders and cinnamon. Add more coffee or milk powder until of thick pouring consistency.

Assembly: To unmould large bombe, dip container briefly in bowl or sink of hot water, then turn out onto serving plate. Place back in freezer to re-chill exterior. Then pour Chocolate or Carob Topping on large or small bombes to cover. Chill for another 5 minutes for small bombes, 15 minutes or more for large one. Garnish as above.

139 *Caramel Cheesecake* SERVES 12

- *40 minutes preparation time* •
- *50 minutes baking time* •
- *8 hours or overnight chilling time* •

This is not a quickie but I couldn't resist including such a fabulous dessert. It is ideal for a large group of dessert-lovers — though by all means precede it with a meal. Pecans and hazelnuts can be used in place of the almonds. Serve in small rich slices.

Cookie Crust

60g butter or margarine

125g wholemeal or gluten-free cookies, crushed

Melt butter and stir in cookie crumbs. Pat into a 23cm springform pan. Chill.

Filling

1¼ cups coarsely chopped almonds
1 tbs butter or margarine
750g cream cheese, at room temperature, or 2 blocks tofu
2 tsp vanilla
3 eggs

¼ cup cream or yoghurt (or if using tofu option: 1½ cups coconut cream)
1 cup brown sugar
3 tbs rice flour or other

Toast almonds in butter. Whizz cream cheese or option, vanilla, egg, and cream or option in a blender until smooth. Pour into a large bowl and stir in sugar, flour and one cup of nuts.

Pour into the springform pan and bake at 180°C for 50 minutes, just until set. Test· with a knife inserted in the centre — it should not be gooey. Cool, then chill thoroughly for one to two hours. Remove from pan.

Caramel Topping

½ cup brown sugar
60g butter or margarine

whipped cream or Tofu Whip for piping and for garnish

Over a low heat cook butter and sugar for about 5 minutes, until brown and thick. Pour on top, not sides, of cake and chill briefly to set. Cover top with remaining nuts. Chill for 6 hours or longer. Cover sides and outer top edge with whipped cream.

Cook's Helper

A WEEK OF SUMMER MENUS

33.
Yellow Rice
Cuban Stewed Vegetables with Meat or option
Peanut and Cauliflower Salad

81.
Potato or Kumara Patties
Mixed Vegetable Hot Pot
Cucumber with Mint Mayonnaise

68.
Antipasto
Pizza Paisano

7.
Summer Soup
Vegetable Platter
Pita Bread or option

107.
Mexicana Chicken or option
Poppyseed Pasta or Corn Chips
Salsa Salad

51.
Egg Foo Yung
Chinese Mushroom Sauce
5-Spice Vegetable Chow Mein

25.
Danish Macaroni Salad with Herring or option
Steamed Beets
Dill Dressing

A WEEK OF WINTER MENUS

88.
Mixed Grill with Tofu or option
Texas Barbecue Sauce
Coleslaw

71.
Nutty Noodle Ring
with Salad Garnish
Saucy Vegetables

108.
Chinese 5-Dragon Kebabs
Lemon Rice
Sesame Spinach Salad

95.
Pumpkin Wedges
Sunflower Topping
German Green Bean Salad

94.
Oriental Roll-ups with Fish or option
Tamarillo Sauce
Vegetables Golden Pagoda

61.
Vegetable Cottage Pie
Tomatoes in Vinaigrette

1.
Cream of Cauliflower Soup
Toasted Almond Topping
Cracker Selection

SUPER QUICK IDEAS FOR ONE

81.• Stuffed Sesame Tomatoes & Courgettes
  • Pasta or Potatoes
  • Parmesan Spinach Salad

68.• Antipasto
  • Pizza Paisano

107.• Mexicana Chicken/Fish/Tofu-Tempeh
  • Poppyseed Pasta or Corn Chips
  • Salsa Salad

96.• Potato Parcels
  • Corn on the Cob
  • Beetroot Salad

108.• Chinese 5-Dragon Kebabs
  • Lemon Rice
  • Sesame Spinach Salad

1.• Cream of Cauliflower Soup
  • Toasted Almond Topping
  • Cracker Selection

19.• Chef's Summer Salad
  • Choice of Dressings & Sauces
  • Corn on the Cob

32.• Bami Goreng
  • Peanut Sauce
  • Cucumber Salad

50.• Spanish Omelette
  • Crispy Potatoes
  • Poppyseed Salad

43.• Corn & Spinach Fritters
  • Kumara (Sweet Potato)
  • Sprout Platter & Tangy Topping

31.• Pasta Perfecto
  • Casentino Walnut Sauce
  • Broccoli Salad

26.• Tacos with myriad accompaniments
  and toppings

88.• Mixed Grill
  • Texas Barbecue Sauce
  • Coleslaw

52.• Avocados Rancheros
  • Corn on the Cob or Steamed Beets
  • Pita Bread or Corn Chips

16.• Brasado al Marsala
  • Crisp Salad

15.• Pumpkin & Tamarillo Stew
  • Puffs
  • Radish Jacks

MENUS FOR ENTERTAINING

119.• Gazpacho
  91.• Port & Peppercorn Pinwheels
    • Paprika Vegetable Medley
    • Bean Sprout Garnish
134.• Carob Crisp with Coffee Cream

113.• Mussel Builders
  31.• Pasta Perfecto
    • Casentino Walnut Sauce
    • Broccoli Salad
139.• Caramel Cheesecake

116.• Bouquet of Asparagus
  92.• Rice Wrappers
    • Coconut Sauce
    • Cauliflower Salad
123.• Glazed Strawberry Flan

117.• Antipasto
  82.• Reuben Rolls
    • Mustard Sauce
    • Baby Carrots with Ginger Glaze
135.• Greek Coffee Cake

110.• Avocado Cream
  94.• Oriental Roll-ups
    • Tamarillo Sauce
    • Vegetables Golden Pagoda
124.• Tropical Cream Pie

109.• Melon & Port
107.• Mexicana Chicken/Fish/Tofu-Tempeh
    • Poppyseed Pasta
    • Salsa Salad
131.• Macaroon Peaches

118.• Baby Corn Consomme
108.• Chinese 5-Dragon Kebabs
    • Lemon Rice
    • Sesame Spinach Salad
138.• Carob-Dipped Ice-Bombe

112.• Tomato Flowers
   2.• Creole Gumbo
    • Cornbread Wedges
    • Avocado Platter
125.• Fruit Platter Pie

111.• Mountain Mushrooms
  32.• Bami Goreng
    • Peanut Sauce
    • Cucumber Sambal & side dishes
127.• Mocha Mousse

114.• Stuffed Grapes
  18.• Stroganoff
    • Noodles or Steamed Kumara
    • Crunchy Salad
      with Tahini Mustard Dressing
126.• Apricot Ginger Mousse

115.• Pears in Tarragon Cream
  49.• Dutch Flatties
    • Capsicum Sauce
    • Cucumber Platter
133.• Marmalade Pudding

see also Special Ethnic Dishes

COOK'S TIPS

The following tips help make cooking easier and more prone to success. And once you understand **processes**, say how rice flour can be used as a thickener, then you can apply this knowledge to your own needs and situations.

Beans (dried), to cook:

Night-before Method
- Soak beans overnight in ample water in large covered saucepan.
- In morning drain off water and replenish; bring water and beans to the boil.
- Boil, partly covered for 30 minutes or longer. Turn off heat and cover pan with a lid and thick towel to trap in the heat and "steam-cook" the beans.
- Leave undisturbed for 40-60 minutes or longer.

On-the-day Method
- In a large saucepan bring ample water to a rolling boil.
- Add beans a handful at a time, so that the water does not stop boiling (this pops their skins enabling them to cook faster).
- Boil for 30 minutes or longer, partly covered (watch for foaming).
- Turn off heat, cover saucepan with lid and towel as above.
- Leave undisturbed for 60 minutes or more.

If you work or otherwise must leave the house during the day and want the beans ready for use upon your return, either of these methods may be employed as long as you allow in your morning schedule for that 30 minutes boiling time. Then turn off the heat, cover as indicated, and leave beans to sit until your return.

Chillies (fresh), how to handle:

The volatile oils of hot chillies may make your skin tingle and eyes burn. Wear rubber gloves if you prefer and be careful not to touch your eyes or face. Do not let children handle chillies. The chilli seeds may be included in your cooking but they are especially hot.

Coconut milk, to prepare:

- Crack open a fresh coconut (shake your coconut before buying, the more liquid inside the fresher it is).
- Pare the brown skin and chop or break the coconut meat into small chunks.
- Measure the chunks and add an equal amount of hot (not boiling) water with it in a blender or food processor. Blend, scrape and blend again until it is a thick fibrous liquid.
- Scrape the mixture into a fine sieve lined with a double thickness of cheesecloth and set over a deep bowl. With a wooden spoon press down hard on the cheesecloth mixture to extract as much liquid as possible. Bring the ends of the cheesecloth together to enclose the pulp and squeeze out any remaining liquid.
- Discard the pulp. One cup of coarsely chopped coconut meat combined with 1 cup hot water should produce 1 cup of coconut milk. Covered and refrigerated the milk will keep for about 5 days, or freeze in small amounts and use as needed.

Lentils and dried peas, to cook:

These may be soaked overnight for quicker cooking. In either case —

- In a saucepan place 1 cup lentils or dried peas to at least 2 cups water or Vegetable Stock; herbs, spices and vegetables may be added.
- Bring to the boil, then simmer partly covered (watch for foaming) for 30-40 minutes (less if soaked).

Rice (brown), to cook:

Never-fail Rice Cooking Method. This produces fluffy brown rice which doesn't stick to the bottom of the pan and is nutritionally superior due to the relatively brief period of high heat used.

- Rinse rice and place in a saucepan.
- Add 1¾ parts water to 1 part rice.
- Cover with lid, bring to the boil, then simmer briskly for 10 minutes (if desired herbs, spices and vegetables may also be added for a one-pot rice dish), otherwise the rice is best left unstirred and covered so as to retain heat and come out fluffy.
- Turn off heat. Cover and surround saucepan with a thick towel to trap in heat and "steam-cook" rice. Be careful to keep the towel away from any hot elements.
- Leave undisturbed for 30 minutes or longer; if off to work, etc, the rice may be cooked, wrapped up, and left until your return.

Rice flour, how to use it:

- As a thickener rice flour is excellent, virtually never going lumpy, and not having that raw taste of wheat flour which needs longer and careful cooking in sauces and custards. Two tablespoons will thicken 1 cup of liquid.
- For lighter, more nourishing baking with wholemeal flour, use half rice flour, half wholemeal flour.
- For gluten-free baking use all rice flour as a binding agent, in cookies, cakes and the like; or use mostly rice flour and part arrowroot, potato flour, soy flour, etc. When making an exchange for wheat or white flour in a recipe just use rice flour measure for measure.

Rice noodles, to cook:

Bring ample water to the boil, then add noodles. Turn off heat, cover with lid, and let sit for 8 minutes. Drain and use.

SUBSTITUTES

To replace eggs

Boiled linseed — boil 1 part ground linseed to 3 parts water for about 3 minutes until thick and gluey. Ample mixture may be made and stored in a covered jar in the refrigerator for several weeks.

To replace 1 egg use 3 tablespoons boiled linseed.

To replace gluten-flours (wheat, rye, oats, cornflour, semolina and barley)

- If you wish to use some wholemeal flour use half rice flour for a higher-rising, lighter-textured product.
- For gluten-free baking use either all rice flour (measure for measure) or at least half rice flour and half pea, soy, arrowroot or potato flour.
- For grain-free baking use a combination of pea, soy, chickpea, potato and/or arrowroot flours.
- To use heavier flours like ground millet or coarse cornmeal use sparingly to say quarter of the total; fine cornmeal or buckwheat flour may be used for up to half the flour called for.
- To replace cornflour use equal amounts arrowroot.

To replace milk

In baking, sauces, custards, etc use soy milk, goat milk, coconut milk, coconut cream. Use measure for measure though coconut cream is very thick and rich and could be thinned.

To replace whipped cream (see also DESSERTS)

As a garnish or for folding into a mousse, pie filling, etc use thick Tofu Whip, Custard (made with milk alternative), sweet sauce or in some cases sweetened fluffy beaten egg white (meringue) or an ice "cream" like Lite-Licks.

To replace cottage or cream cheese

In a dessert recipe like cheesecake, use thick Sweet Tofu Whip to achieve an equivalent density. In savoury recipes use Savoury Tofu Whip.

To replace butter

In cakes, cookies and the like, exchange measure for measure for cold-pressed oil. The oil will be too oily in batters where the butter is a dominant ingredient as with shortbread or pound cake.

To replace sugar

In baking use about half the amount of honey, or estimate that ¼-½ cup of honey will sweeten an average 23cm cake; if there is considerable liquid in the batter, decrease this by ¼ cup for every ½ cup of honey used.

When changing a recipe from sugar to honey, if more than ½ cup honey is used, lower oven temperature by 20°C to prevent overbrowning.

Measure the honey for your recipe in the same cup first used to measure the oil called for — it will slip out effortlessly.

Toasting, nuts and seeds

- Place in a sturdy frypan (such as cast-iron) and toast without oil over a low-medium heat until of desired light-medium brown colour. Stir frequently.
- Or place on a tray and toast in low-medium oven for 10-20 minutes or until well done. Stir frequently.

GLOSSARY

- **Agar** is a seaweed-based setting agent similar to gelatine in use. It is protein and calcium rich and easy to digest. There are two forms: granulated, more processed but cheaper and stronger acting, 1 tsp sets one cup of liquid; and flakes, 1 tbs sets 1 cup of liquid. For both forms, bring agar and some or all of the liquid to the boil and simmer for one minute. Use as required. Agar sets very quickly, even while it is warm. If it sets before you are ready it may be lightly reheated to liquefy it without adverse effect.

- **Apple Cider Vinegar** is usually recommended, as opposed to other types of vinegar, because it is naturally rather than artificially fermented. Its mild taste is suitable for all types of salad dressings and for drinks (try 1-3 tsp with or without honey in warm water).

- **Arrowroot** is a natural thickening agent. Ground from dried root of a tropical plant, it is easy to digest, and a good protein source. One to 1½ tbs thickens 1 cup liquid.

- **Buckwheat** is a small, almost triangular-shaped "grain" (actually a member of the rhubarb family), popular in the Middle East. Treat it like rice, its nutty flavour enhances soups, savoury mixtures, pilafs, and cooked breakfast cereals; is gluten free. Buckwheat flour is also available.

- **Carob.** Rich, sweet, nourishing carob pods are de-seeded, toasted and ground into a fine powder known as carob flour or carob powder. Carob can be used in place of cocoa, just use about a third more carob; say 4 tbs carob to replace 3 tbs cocoa.

- **Cereal-Coffee** usually contains a blend of roasted vegetables, roots, beans (not coffee beans) and grains such as barley and rye (those on gluten-free diets take note). They contain no caffeine and look, prepare and taste similar to ordinary coffee (see also **Dandelion Coffee**). Ordinary coffee raises blood pressure, over-stimulates bowels, kidneys, liver, irritates stomach lining, destroys B vitamins, prevents iron absorption, aggravates heart, arterial and nervous disorders.

- **Chickpeas** are also called garbanzo beans. High in protein, they should be cooked as for other beans; may be cooked and ground for dips and savoury mixtures. Chickpeas are also ground into flour and used as a savoury-binding agent and in small proportions in baking.

- **Chocolate** is a preparation made from cacao seeds which are naturally bitter. It requires considerable fat and sugar to produce the sweet and creamy substance alluring to so many. Chocolate contains caffeine and other central nervous system stimulants such as theobromine which artificially speeds heartbeat. Another component — oxalic acid — interferes with calcium absorption. See **Carob** for alternatives.

- **Coconut** is a good source of phosphorous and potassium. Many brands of coconut are sweetened with sugar, but the desiccated form is usually superior.

- **Cold-pressed oils** are those in which the oil is extracted using little or no heat or chemical solvents. These oils are best kept refrigerated.

- **Crudites** is a French term for raw vegetables to nibble on, as used for vegetable platters.

- **Dahl,** or dal, is the Hindi name for all legumes and pulses. In the West it has become a general heading for a variety of dried peas.

- **Dandelion Coffee** is prepared from roasted ground dandelion root. Both instant and percolator varieties are available. It is rich in nutrients and beneficially increases activity in the liver, pancreas and spleen — unlike the harsh action of ordinary coffee.

- **Ghee** is clarified butter which doesn't burn over a high heat and has a distinctive nutty flavour. Available at major foodstores, ghee is used in Indian cooking.

- **Gluten** is a protein element in certain grains: wheat, rye, oats and barley. Non-gluten containing grains are: rice, cornmeal, millet, buckwheat. For baking and thickening purposes there are also the following flours: soy, chickpea, arrowroot, potato.

- **Herb Salt** usually contains seasalt, but in varying proportion to the accompanying herbs, spices, yeast, etc. One currently available brand — "Vegit" — contains no salt at all.

- **Julienne** refers to matchstick-size pieces as when slicing carrots, celery, potato, etc.

- **Kelp** is one of the richest sources of iodine, crucial for the health of the thyroid gland; it is also rich in Vitamin B and E, and like other seaweeds rich in minerals. It comes in powder, granules or tablets, and may be sprinkled on foods as for salt.

- **Legumes** are a pod-type of vegetable such as dried peas, beans and lentils. They are a good source of protein, complex carbohydrate and many vitamins and minerals.

- **Liquid Chlorophyll** is a commercially available product derived from alfalfa. It is particularly alkaline, a blood purifier, nutrient and enzyme rich. Mildly flavoured with natural mint essence, it is also a safe green food colouring agent in desserts and drinks.

- **Margarine**. See COMMERCIAL PRODUCTS list following.

- **Miso** is a Japanese seasoning paste like marmite in colour, texture and taste. It is made from a fermentation of soybeans, salt and water; some varieties may contain rice or barley. Use as a nutritious spread or to flavour soups, sauces and the like.

- **Molasses**, the last extraction of the cane in refining sugar, is rich in iron, calcium, potassium, B vitamins and other nutrients. It provides moisture, colour and flavour in cooking.

- **Nuts and Seeds**. Nuts are the dried fruits or seeds of plants; seeds are the nutrient-laden ripened ovule of plants. They contain protein, unsaturated fats, vitamins A, B, D and E, phosphorous, calcium, zinc, magnesium, potassium, iodine. Sesame seeds are particularly rich in calcium; pumpkin kernels in zinc; and sunflower seeds are up to 50 per cent protein. Unhulled seeds may be stored in a cool, dark place in a covered container. Hulled nuts and seeds should be refrigerated and used promptly, otherwise the oxidation of their fat content will make them go rancid. Nuts and seeds must be chewed thoroughly or they will interfere with digestion.

- **Puree**. To puree cooked vegetables, soaked dried fruits, etc either whizz in blender or put through a food mill.

- **Seaweed** is an ocean vegetable, rich in all minerals and helpful in maintaining health of mucous membranes. To use, soak 3-5cm for a few minutes in warm water to soften, drain and chop. Add to soups, stews, rice dishes and salads.

- **Semolina** is a type of wheat cereal or flour.

- **Tahini** is a nut butter similar in appearance to peanut butter. It is made from roasted ground sesame seeds and oil. Use as a spread, topping, in dips, dressings, sauces, soups.

- **Tea** contains caffeine and is a stimulant like coffee. The tannin has harmful effects on the mucous membrane of the mouth and digestive tract. There are a wide range of herb tea alternatives.

- **Tofu and Tempeh**. Tofu or bean curd or soy cheese is made by adding a natural coagulant like lemon juice or nigari (of seaweed base) to soymilk — much like the process of making yoghurt. It then develops curds and is pressed to remove excess liquid. A semi-solid white "cake" results. Tofu is soft, easy to digest, a valuable protein and calcium source, and a cook's delight due to its blandness — for it can thus take on a sweet or savoury personality and quickly absorbs the colour and flavour of the foods it is blended with. In terms of flavour and usability think of it like a block of compressed cottage cheese. Like cottage cheese it can be used in desserts, main dishes, dips, etc.

  Tempeh is cultured from cooked, split soybeans much the same way as if making cheese. The beans are mixed with a tempeh starter and allowed to rest in a warm place overnight. The tempeh mould partially breaks down protein during fermentation making it highly digestible. A solid white cake forms which is mild tasting though with a cheesy richness denser than tofu. It is quick cooking and ideal baked, grilled, fried or added to stews and casseroles.

- **Vegetable Stock** is made by collecting liquid remaining after steaming vegetables, or by simmering vegetables and water, then straining and using as required. A nutritious, flavourful addition to soups, sauces, dressings, savoury mixtures, stews and rice dishes.

- **Vinaigrette** is a simple oil and vinegar dressing from which many variations stem. The traditional proportion is three parts oil to one part vinegar.

- **Yeast**. Food Yeast or Nutritional Yeast, cultured on molasses, is used as a food supplement. It is rich in protein, vitamins and minerals and its taste is mild, savoury, nutty. Comvita brand is a tasty unsalted variety. Like many other "good" foods however, yeast like wheat and milk is another common allergen.

  Brewer's Yeast is cultured on barley. It too is nourishing like food yeast but has a strong, often bitter taste.

- **Yeast**, to prepare: Baker's Yeast or live yeast in cake form or granulated is used as a leavener. To prepare granulated yeast: Place a small bowl in a warm place (such as on a burner turned briefly to low); in it dissolve ¼ tsp honey in 3 tbs hot water (too cool and the yeast won't grow; too hot and it will be killed). Sprinkle with 1 tbs granulated yeast. Stir lightly then leave to froth and prove 5-10 minutes. If it does not rise the yeast is either inactive (check the expiry date on the jar) or the water temperature was not right.

EQUIPMENT

- **Bain-marie** is a shallow pan filled with water into which smaller pans are placed. Food thus cooks evenly and without boiling or achieving a too crisp exterior. The method is suitable, for example, for a baked custard.

- **Blender and Food Processor** are invaluable aids in the kitchen, especially for natural foods cooking. They are used to puree, chop, mash, blend, and to prepare drinks, sauces, dressings, savoury mixtures, desserts and much more. Buy a good quality machine, it is well worth it.

- **Bundt Pan** is a decorative cake pan with a rounded, ribbed bottom.

- **Double Boiler** is useful for delicate sauces, custards, and frostings. It is traditionally a two-saucepan unit: the bottom saucepan simmers the water, while the second saucepan (containing the mixture to be cooked) fits inside the bottom pan so as to elevate and cook the mixture above the water. A two-saucepan-style steamer unit may "double" as a double boiler: place pan with perforated holes on top of base saucepan as usual. Place a stainless steel bowl inside the top pan to contain your mixture. Fill bottom unit with water and steam over a medium heat.

- **Knives** should be sharp, substantial, and good to hold as they are crucial to a cook's craft. Again, buy quality, keep knives sharp and learn to use the right knife for the right purpose.

- **Springform Pan** is one with sides which loosen to pull apart from the base.

- **Steamers** elevate food away from the water below so as to retain nutrients, colour, and texture. The remaining liquid should be reserved and used within the week as a vegetable stock for soups, sauces, cooking rice, etc. Two basic types of steamers are available: a two-part saucepan unit with top pot having a base with perforated holes; and, a steamer-insert which is collapsible and made of stainless steel. This fits into any size saucepan, has a central "handle" for easy lifting, and is reasonably priced.

N.B. The use of aluminium cookware is not advisable, as the metal is unstable and cooks into food (as does the base metal of non-stick coatings, once scratched). Recommended is stainless steel, cast-iron, glass and pottery.

COMMERCIAL PRODUCTS
SUITED TO SPECIAL DIETS

Some suggestions for easy snacks and meal extenders using purchased prepared foods. These are a boon for those on special diets, for children, and anyone interested in variety considering our western culture's habitual use of milk and gluten.

- **Banana chips**. Thin slices of banana, dried then toasted with honey.

- **Bread**. Cornbread by Mamata Bakery, Grey Lynn, Auckland; the wide range of Vitalia breads available at delicatessens and health food stores.

- **Cake**. Fruit cake from Muffin Bakehouse. Cakes and cookies from Mamata Bakery, Auckland.

- **Cereals, puffed**. Blackmores' Abundant Earth range of puffed whole grain cereals roughly resemble rice bubbles but are made from brown rice and other whole grains minus the customary sugar and salt. Varieties: rice, millet, corn. These can be served as breakfast cereals or snack nibbles, or toasted and seasoned as croutons for soups, snacks, salads, curries and the like.

- **Cheese**. Goat's milk feta and goat's milk camembert; sheep's milk feta. Beware that feta is very salty. Nice in cooking, however, where a little bit can flavour a large lasagne or similar dish. Roquefort is also made from sheep's milk but is very expensive.

- **Coconut cream**. A tinned product from Samoa which is widely available. It contains emulsifier but is a handy, rich, creamy treat for those on milk-free diets. It has a mild sweet coconut flavour which is overpowered with the addition of other seasonings and so works just fine in savoury casseroles, sauces, etc.

- **Cookies**. Blackmores' Abundant Earth gluten-free and/or milk-free range: carob, honey, oat, and peanut butter. Also Healtheries gluten-free (but not milk-free) cookie range.

- **Corn chips**. "Sancho" is a less salty brand than most and one with no chemical additives.

- **Crackers**. Rice crackers from Healtheries; two varieties: thick and round, thin and rectangular. Also rice crackers from Westbrae with many flavours like sesame, onion, seaweed, etc. For wheat-free rather than gluten-free diets: Kavli rye crackers.

- **Drinks**. Naturally flavoured soymilk drinks in cartons (some brands contain barley); also carob powder, dandelion coffee, individual sachets of miso soup, herb tea, fruit juice.

- **Ice cream**. Soy-based Lite-licks is delicious and currently in five flavours. Also goat's milk ice cream in several flavours. All available from major foodstores.

- **Margarine**. Most margarines contain cheap hydrogenated oils, milk solids, artificial colourings and preservatives. Two current brands to the contrary: Vi-tal, and Slimarine which is much saltier.

HERBS AND SPICES

The effective use of herbs and spices readily transforms adequate fare into exciting dining. Note that dried herbs are three to four times more powerful in flavour than fresh herbs.

- **Allspice** — dried pod, whole or powdered. Use sparingly in cakes, when simmering dried fruit. Also good in savoury brown or tomato sauces as a peppery touch. Complements carob dishes.
- **Aniseed** — seeds or powder (anise). Sweet liquorice aroma and taste. For biscuits, cakes, Chinese cooking.
- **Basil or Sweet Basil** — leaves or ground. Mild, sweet may be used generously in sauces, fish, savoury mixtures, dressings, soups, vegetables.
- **Bay Leaf** — leaves or ground. For stews, soups, sauces, fish, tomato dishes.
- **Caraway** — seed. Strong, pungent. For breads, cakes, cabbage, dressings.
- **Cardamom** — pod or ground. For hot drinks, cakes, rice, curries, fish, stews, fruit salad.
- **Cayenne** — ground peppers. Many varieties and degrees of hotness. For beans, dressings, sauces, table condiment.
- **Celery Seed** — seeds or ground. For salad dressings, soups, stews, stuffings.
- **Chervil** — leaves similar to parsley. Delicate liquorice flavour, good with bland foods like eggs, fish, salads, soups.
- **Chives** — leaves. For garnishing or adding just before serving (too delicate to be overcooked). For spreads, dips, salads, fish, tomatoes.
- **Cinnamon** — stick or ground. Sweet and spicy. For hot drinks, desserts, baked goods, tomato sauce, with carob.
- **Cloves** — whole buds or ground. Sharp and spicy. For pies, baked goods, hot drinks, apple, pear, banana and other fruit desserts.
- **Coriander** — seeds or ground. For stews, sauces, dips, dressings, vegetables, rice, apple and pumpkin pies, baked goods.
- **Cumin** — seeds or ground. Spicy, slightly sweet flavour. For beans, sauces, stews, dips, salad dressings.
- **Dill** — leaf or seed. Fresh dill has a magnificent, cleansing aroma and taste. For creamy soups, spreads, fish, salads, potatoes.
- **Fennel** — whole or ground. Faint liquorice taste. For cakes, cookies, bread, soups, stews, rice, fish, mayonnaise.
- **Garam Masala** — a blend of several spices such as cumin, cardamom, turmeric, cinnamon and others. Sweet, mildly spicy flavour.
- **Garlic** — bulb or powder. Sweet, pungent. For vegetables, sauces, salads, beans, soups, stews, dressings.
- **Ginger** — root. Peel root before using. Sweet, spicy. For rice, vegetables, sauces, soups, hot drinks, baked goods, dressings.
- **Horseradish** — dried root and powder. Hot, tangy. For sauces and dressings.
- **Juniper** — berries. Faint gin smell. For fish, stews.
- **Lemon Verbena** — leaf. Lemon flavour. For fish, sauces, stews, stuffings.

- **Marjoram** — leaves and stems. For salads, dressings, fish, stuffing, savoury mixtures, stews.
- **Mint** — leaves fresh or dried. For garnishes, drinks, salads, dressings.
- **Mustard** — seeds or powder. Pungent. For sauces, dressings.
- **Nasturtium** — leaves, sweet, peppery. For salads, garnish.
- **Nutmeg** — seeds or powder. For baked goods, hot drinks, sauces, stews, carrots.
- **Oreganum** — leaves or ground. "Mediterranean" taste. Use generously in soups, stews, with beans, fish, dressings, tomatoes.
- **Paprika** — powdered red pepper. Provides colour and mildly sweet taste. For dark sauces, dressings, mayonnaise, potatoes, beans, garnish.
- **Parsley** — leaves and stems, fresh or dried. Good in just about everything savoury; garnish.
- **Poppy Seeds** — whole seeds. Sweet, nut-like. For baked goods, desserts, fillings and sauces. Garnish for sweets, vegetables and things savoury.
- **Rosemary** — needle-like leaves. Strong flavour. For fish, beans, stuffings, savoury mixtures.
- **Saffron** — flower and stalk, whole or ground. Distinctive flavour and amber colour. For rice, curries, vegetables, cakes, cookies.
- **Sage** — leaf or ground, several varieties. Strong, aromatic. For stuffings, eggs, stews, beans, savoury mixtures.
- **Savoury** — leaves or ground, use sparingly. Popular French herb, thyme-like smell. For eggs, fish, stuffings, rice, stews.
- **Tarragon** — leaves, for delicate dishes. For salads, eggs, fish, dressings, soups, savoury mixtures.
- **Thyme** — leaves or ground. Strong smell (try lemon thyme) for grains, stews, beans, potatoes.
- **Turmeric** — ground. Bright golden colour, sharp taste. Use sparingly. Beautifully colours rice and grains; vegetables, soups, sauces, spreads.
- **Vanilla** — pod or ground, or essence. Essence may be pure, mixed or wholly synthetic (one quality brand is Healthways "Natural Vanilla Extract"). Pods may be used to flavour liquid, dried and re-used.

Index

All figures refer to recipes unless otherwise indicated. Bold entries are section headings.